Kundalini Awakening

2 Books in 1: Open Your Third Eye, Increase Psychic Abilities, Expand Mind Power, Astral Travel, Attain Higher Consciousness and Spiritual Enlightenment

Laura Connelly

© Copyright 2020 by Laura Connelly. All right reserved.

The work contained herein has been produced with the intent to provide relevant knowledge and information on the topic on the topic described in the title for entertainment purposes only. While the author has gone to every extent to furnish up to date and true information, no claims can be made as to its accuracy or validity as the author has made no claims to be an expert on this topic. Notwithstanding, the reader is asked to do their own research and consult any subject matter experts they deem necessary to ensure the quality and accuracy of the material presented herein.

This statement is legally binding as deemed by the Committee of Publishers Association and the American Bar Association for the territory of the United States. Other jurisdictions may apply their own legal statutes. Any reproduction, transmission or copying of this material contained in this work without the express written consent of the copyright holder shall be deemed as a copyright violation as per the current legislation in force on the date of publishing and subsequent time thereafter. All additional works derived from this material may be claimed by the holder of this copyright.

The data, depictions, events, descriptions and all other information forthwith are considered to be true, fair and accurate unless the work is expressly described as a work of fiction. Regardless of the nature of this work, the Publisher is exempt from any responsibility of actions taken by the reader in conjunction with this work. The Publisher acknowledges that the reader acts of their own accord and releases the author and Publisher of any responsibility for the observance of tips, advice, counsel, strategies and techniques that may be offered in this volume.

TABLE OF CONTENTS

Kundalini and the Chakras

Open Your Third Eye Through Self-Healing Techniques and Learn How to Balance and Unblock Your Chakras

Introduction 2

Chapter 1 *What Is Kundalini* 3

Chapter 2 *Awakening The Kundalini* 9

Chapter 3 *Accessing Kundalini Through Open Chakras* 22

Chapter 4 *Signs Your Kundalini Is Awakened* 34

Chapter 5 *Your Metamorphosis In Four Stages* 53

Chapter 6 *Life After Kundalini Awakening* 60

Chapter 7 *Methods For Awakening The Kundalini* 64

Conclusion 72

Kundalini

Ultimate Guide to Awaken Your Third Eye Chakra, Develop Awareness and Spiritual Power Through Kundalini and Chakra Awakening

Introduction 74

Chapter 1 *The Third Eye Chakra* 75

Chapter 2 *The Third Eye And Psychic Abilities* 80

Chapter 3 *Exploring The Spirit World* 89

Chapter 4 *Seeing Other Worlds Through The Third Eye* 98

Chapter 5 *Opening Your Third Eye Chakra* 107

Chapter 6 *The Pineal Gland And The Third Eye* 122

Chapter 7 *Reiki Healing And The Third Eye* 128

Chapter 8 *Psychic Abilities And Your Third Eye* 130

Conclusion 148

Kundalini and the Chakras

Open Your Third Eye Through Self-Healing Techniques and Learn How to Balance and Unblock Your Chakras

Laura Connelly

INTRODUCTION

Congratulations on purchasing *Kundalini and the Chakras,* and thank you for doing so.

The following chapters will discuss the incredible journey you are about to embark on as you begin to learn the knowledge that you need to know about the Kundalini and how to awaken it inside of you. You will soon see where the Kundalini comes from and what it feels like when yours begins to awaken. You will learn how to balance your Kundalini as it begins to stimulate and how you can support it while you are developing your Kundalini.

You are about to begin a journey that will change your life. With your Kundalini in action, your life will be nothing like it was before. You will discover a power inside of you that you never knew existed, and that power can transform your life, once you have learned what it is and what to do with it.

Kundalini is a potential force that lives inside of everyone, a dormant yet powerful force waiting to be awakened and utilized. This energy from the divine will be the strongest when you are spiritual and energetic, and these are things that are possible when you awaken your Kundalini.

There are plenty of books on this subject on the market; thanks so much again for choosing this one! Every possible effort has been made to ensure that it is full of as much useful information as possible, so please enjoy!

CHAPTER 1
What Is Kundalini

Kundalini comes from ancient India, and it is a term that identifies the awakening and arising of consciousness and an energy that is waiting coiled at the base of your spine. This power has been waiting there since you were born. It is the source of the force that drives your life. Ancient beliefs say that this power causes the formation of the baby in the mother's womb, and then it coils itself at the base of the spine of the fetus, growing as the baby grew. The power then lies at the bottom of the spine, waiting to be unlocked, awakened, and utilized until it uncoils and returns to its source when you die.

The Energy and Consciousness of Kundalini

Kundalini is an energy that you can gain when you make a meditative and focused effort. It will provide you with a state of blissful consciousness when you have awakened it. You will uncoil the Kundalini and bring it up through all of the seven internal chakras until it reaches the Crown Chakra and affects its function. When you awaken the Kundalini inside yourself, then you will know the joy of total enlightenment.

Kundalini is a spiritual and psychological energy that animates your consciousness. It lies dormant in your sleeping body, and you can arouse it through the use of many different methods to bring new states of consciousness to yourself. When you can experience the power of Kundalini, you will feel energy like none you have ever felt before.

Most people are not aware of their own conscious and psychic abilities. Some realms lay far beyond the physical world you inhabit, and you have spiritual abilities you don't yet realize. Kundalini has been a universal phenomenon for centuries. It was often written about in the teachings of the mystics living in cultures around the world, especially those in the Far East. These people knew about the power of Kundalini and have taught others how to unlock the power down through the generations.

While there is writing on how to awaken the Kundalini rapidly, it is far better to do the awakening slowly and purposefully. An explosive awakening might be too much for your system to handle. You will want to bring the Kundalini to your Crown Chakra, but this ascension should be gradual and purposeful. If you were suddenly transported to the fifth dimension of reality, you would find that it is too different from the truth that you are used to and impossible to understand. You would want to be brought home suddenly, but then you might find your dimension to be dull and boring. In the same way, you do not want to awaken your Kundalini too rapidly because you might find the sudden levels of energy and enlightenment too much for you to handle all at once. Take your awakening slowly, because getting your Kundalini ascended to your Crown Chakra is not an ultimate goal but a part of your journey.

Awakening the Kundalini gradually will give you the power to enjoy yourself and to enjoy the love you will share with others who are on the same journey. You will eventually realize that all man shares one consciousness and that the process of awakening your Kundalini will bring you to this understanding. When you have elevated your spirituality to a higher vibration, you will have a sharper perception of your oneness with the universe. When you awaken your Kundalini, it will rise through the six internal chakras until it reaches the Crown Chakra. It will awaken even more as it rises through all of the levels of the chakras. When the energized Kundalini reaches the Crown Chakra, it will produce a profound transformation of revolutionary consciousness. Your mental eye will begin to see super sensual visions. Charming sights and new worlds that are full of incredible wonders will show themselves to you. You will receive power and energy and divine knowledge in ever-increasing degrees as your Kundalini brings your chakras to life as it passes through on its way to the Crown Chakra.

Location of the Kundalini

Everyone has two distinct bodies, the subtle body and the gross body. The gross body is the one you can feel and see. It is made of your limbs, torso, head, and inner organs; it is all of the physical parts of you. Your subtle body is that part of you that thinks and reasons and feels. Your Kundalini resides in your subtle body. The subtle body is made of subtle energy, psychic centers, channels of power, and drops of essence that all work together to keep your subtle body functioning.

The Kundalini is coiled in three and one-half coils at the base of your spine. Two currents of nerves run through your spinal column, and a hollow canal runs through your spinal cord. At the bottom of the open channel in the spinal cord is the Lotus of the Kundalini. This structure is a triangular-shaped mass of matter that holds the coiled power of the Kundalini. When the Kundalini is awakened, it will rise through the six lower chakras through the passage of the hollow canal in the spinal cord. As the Kundalini rises through the chakras, it will liberate another layer of your mind, causing them to become open so that you will begin to realize the beautiful powers from the different visions.

The spinal cord is created strangely. Imagine a figure eight lying down horizontally. The two parts of the figure-eight meet in the middle, and this makes the hollow channel through which the Kundalini travels. Envision many figure eights, all laying down, one on top of the other, all the way down your back. The parts that meet in the middle area are hollow. As the Kundalini begins to uncoil and awaken, it will travel slowly upward through the channel.

Purpose of the Kundalini

The Kundalini is an intelligent force, coursing through your body energetically. When the Kundalini first begins to awaken, it begins to travel up the hollow channel in the center of the spine. When the Kundalini first begins to awaken, it can be very energetic and somewhat fierce. When you activate your energy in your body, it can quickly awaken the material you have stored in your chakras. You might feel electrical sensations running like currents up your spine as your experiences and emotions grow more intense with time. Until you learn to control the surge of energy accurately, the Kundalini might feel like a small volcano surging up your spine as it starts to awaken and move.

Kundalini, as a life force, is inexhaustible. When you begin to awaken the Kundalini inside of you, you will become sensitive to the vibrational energies it will give off. As your perception becomes more enhanced, your prevailing wisdom regarding life will begin to deepen and strengthen. When your perception is increased, you will start to enjoy a more in-depth understanding of life and your position in the universe. As you gain new knowledge of life and the experiences you have, you will also be feeding your Kundalini your energy. With all of the knowledge you are gathering comes clarity, and with this clarity comes more awakening. All of this clarity will help to build up energy in your Kundalini, and this will need to be directed toward something useful.

The energy you have gathered will be used to awaken and energize the first six internal chakras as the Kundalini travels toward the Crown Chakra. The Kundalini will always direct excess energy upward. Your system of inner chakras is just like a circuit of energy systems that are all powered with one course of electricity. This circuit of power travels up your spine using the power from the Kundalini. Your awakening Kundalini will continue to work its way up to your spine until it meets some blockage that stops its progress. It will usually find a blockage in one of the first three chakras where you hold the emotions of your family issues, deep emotions, and your ancestry and past. As the energy builds behind the blockage, it will eventually break through and release the blockage from that chakra so that the Kundalini can continue on its path. Kundalini is intelligent, and it will create its cycles of rising and falling. It will travel as far as it possibly can until it encounters a blockage it can't break through. Then the Kundalini will retreat to the Root Chakra, the chakra at the base of the spine, and it will wait there until it has built up enough energy to continue in its mission. Then it will rise up through the chakras again, going further upward each time. Eventually, the Kundalini will make a complete path to the Crown Chakra, and it will create a complete circuit.

When the energy from the Kundalini has opened the lower six chakras, it will then reach the Crown Chakra, which is its mission. When this happens, you might feel a burst of energy that will travel from your Root Chakra up your spine to your Crown Chakra. Then the Kundalini will rise out of the Crown Chakra in a process that many people find exhilarating and disorienting at the same time. You will feel numerous spiritual, mental, and physical changes all in a brief period. The Kundalini will continue to arise over and over through the central channel. Depending on the power that is needed at the moment, this rising will either feel like an intense rush or a gentle wave. Kundalini is your conscious energy that will do what you need. You might need to clean out large amounts of material from your central column with a boost of energy from your Kundalini. You might need your Kundalini to simmer in your Root chakra while it clears out all of the deep dark issues that are stored there.

Once the Kundalini reaches the Crown Chakra, you will feel a bubble of energy surrounding your Crown Chakra. This bubble will begin to expand with all of the new experiences that you will gain, and it will give you the ultimate access to all of the chakras that hover above and around your head, the chakras that are not part of any human and driven by the divine. This access will consequently allow you to open the chakras beneath your feet. You will begin to realize your humanity as you enjoy your own spiritual and physical self. You will start to see things in shades of gray and not just light and dark. Once your upper chakras, and especially your Crown Chakra, are opened, you will begin to explore your lower chakras and feel comfortable in your own emotional and primal energies and desires. You will be completely open in yourself and to yourself.

The Ultimate Life Force of the Kundalini

When your Kundalini is awakened, it becomes the basis of all that is creative within you. All significant accomplishments, such as those attributed to grace, talent, creativity, or genius. When the Kundalini is awakened, it not only inspires yogis and shamans, but it also inspires mathematicians, composers, artists, and poets. While those involved in the creative arts will be grateful for the impetus given by the Kundalini, it is the shamans and the yogis who will fully understand and completely revere the fully awakened Kundalini. They will see it as the vessel that will carry the select few followers on to the ultimate aim of all life, the goal of self-realization.

The discipline of Hatha Yoga first described the abundance of life force in the Kundalini somewhere near fifteen centuries ago. It was initially thought of as a science whose ultimate goal was to lead to the growth and ascent of the Kundalini and the power it brings to you. The ancient scriptures pointed to the necessity of meditation along with kriya (action), bandha (body strength), pranayama (breathing), and asanas (yoga) to achieve pure Kundalini awareness and spiritual enlightenment. Beyond the physical practices that are needed to awaken the Kundalini, there are also the spiritual practices of yajna (fire worship), bhakti (devotional worship), and mantra (repeated sound) to assist in awakening the Kundalini. Using the physical and spiritual practices that are dedicated to awakening the Kundalini is the most profound of all the ancient teachings.

You want to awaken your Kundalini. You want to be vibrant and alive, and totally in sync with the world around you and the larger universe. You want your spirit, body, and mind to be connected, with those around you, with the people of the world, and with the universe. With the more extensive source of energy, you will receive from an awakened Kundalini, you will be able to the infinity of yourself and your nature. The power you receive from the Kundalini is the source of your creativity and wisdom. When you begin to awaken your Kundalini, you also start to awaken the divine power that is within everyone; you will see the light of your own true consciousness.

Kundalini will provide you with spiritual benefits that you will be able to feel on the physical plane and the etheric planes of the universe. As the dominant force of your Kundalini arises, it will bring strength to your well-being and your vitality. The energy will also allow you to expand your consciousness while it enhances your capacity for personal fulfillment and ultimate joy. Kundalini is not only a highly powerful spiritual system, but it is also a therapeutic practice. It will give you transformation and awakening. Your outlook on life, along with your attitudes and moods, are all driven by the light that shines out from within you. It is the radiance that real awakening will bring to you.

Your mind is the root of all of your distress. The modern lifestyle most people follow makes it too easy to fall into negative patterns of thought that pull all of the vital energy from your heart and soul. This energy is the life force that permeates all creatures and is needed to sustain life. Negative thoughts cause blockages and dysfunction in your energy system. This negativity will lead you to feel tired and disinterested. Awakening your Kundalini will give you the tools that you need to energize your systems and command your mind and body. You will be able to live more consciously as your moods and emotions are governed more effectively. Awakening your Kundalini is the peak of your spiritual progress. It aligns your inner awareness with an awareness of the divine. When your Kundalini is adequately awakened, you will achieve the ultimate freedom.

CHAPTER 2
Awakening The Kundalini

The ultimate life force in your subtle body is the Kundalini. It is your inner fire and your creative power. Once this power is activated, it is timeless and electric, and it can be paralyzing. When you start the energy, it will flow through you in the wavy shape of the serpent to which it is compared. It curves up from the base of your spine, through your gut, past your heart, and into your head. As the energy of the Kundalini flows through this channel, it will pass through all of your chakras and give them a boost of energy to activate them. The Kundalini and the chakras are both found in your subtle body. Life will pass to the Crown Chakra at the top of your head, thus providing you with an expanded state of consciousness.

Kundalini awakening will awaken the dormant energy that resides in your subtle body. You will be able to see the world with an expanded vision. You will have a keen sense of perception that will allow you to combine numerous perspectives all at once. You will be able to understand all of your feelings correctly. You will also become a master at sensing what other people are feeling and how they see the world. This is some of the enlightenment that you will achieve through awakening your Kundalini.

The comparison of the Kundalini to a sleeping serpent comes from the story of Shakti and Shiva. In the information, a resting snake that is coiled eight times is waiting at the bottom of a great mountain to unleash its magnificent power. The Goddess Shakti wants to be with Lord Shiva. Shakti is the force behind all of creation, resting at the base of the spine as she longs to rise and be one with your consciousness at the heights of your spiritual bliss. Shiva is the consciousness of the unmovable power. As Shakti dances for Shiva, he spends significant amounts of time ignoring her, waiting for that moment when he is sure that her desire to be with him is real. Only then will he join her dance, and all of creation will unfold as they dance together. Their union together creates all that is in nature.

Your consciousness sees all of this as it unfolds. The witness in your subtle body is the Shiva, and the nature of the world around you is the Shakti. When the two are separate, you can't achieve spiritual awakening. When Shakti and Shiva merge, it will create the spiritual channel of oneness that the Kundalini will flow through. This is where you will achieve true happiness, and it can't be achieved while we are not united with the world we live in. This state of happiness is not conditional on your life, playing out in any particular pattern. The oneness and unconditional bliss that you will feel can only be achieved when you are at one with all people and all things in nature. You will not be separate from anything in creation.

Kundalini awakening is the concentrated energy of attention or awareness. It is the energy that manifests when your consciousness becomes free from all thought. You will experience more profound feelings of empathy with others. You will discover that you are more sensitive to the needs of others. You will know things profoundly, and you will probably develop psychic abilities. You will have more energy, and the aging process will most likely slow in your body and mind. You will have internal knowing and great peace as your charisma and creativity increase. As you become more of a part of all that is, you will see that all of the great mysteries of life aren't all that mysterious.

Realign your Prana (Life Force)

Your body is made up of pathways through which your energy flows and moves. The point that flows through these pathways is your prana, your life force. You will be able to harness this life force as you learn to awaken and control your Kundalini. This energy can be used to support you and heal you. It works on all levels, spiritually, physically, emotionally, and mentally. Power is a universal concept among all people. It is the undeniable force that allows for the existence of life and allows life to flourish. Western thinking people do not often embrace the concept of energy as it pertains to life and health. Many of the ancient health practices of Eastern medicine use power as a remedy for common physical and mental ailments. It can be used to supplement the most prescribed medications that are already known to work to restore health. This is known as energy healing, and it is the best way to realign your life force.

Depending on the method that you use, healing with energy focuses on the force of life that flows through everyone. This force dictates your ability to connect with other people as well as your strength, health, and mood. In some cultures, this energy is called qi or ki, pronounced as *chee*. Some cultures refer to it as prana. However, it is called; it is the supernatural force that cannot be seen or comprehended in the sense of worldly things. Western medicine and science are beginning to be more receptive to the idea of energy as a method of healing. They are beginning to embrace the principles behind the benefits and techniques that eastern cultures have been using for centuries. Your body runs on energy for every function it does, and your body is made of life. There is also a field of energy that surrounds every person. Being able to influence the flow of energy by using mental intention and awareness and physical abilities will bring you profound results. Your energy body can be altered through exercise, physical touch, and meditation to give you higher levels of energy, consciousness, and health. Techniques for healing your life will help you find the correct approach for you that will lead you on the right path to sustained health and healing.

Qigong – The concept of qi has led to a fundamental practice of energy exercise and healing that is known as qigong. This practice balances the flow of energy through the entire body by using meditation, breathing, and body postures to cultivate the force of life. Since it helps to develop muscle strength and agility, and balance, it is often used as a foundation practice for many of the martial arts disciplines. People who practice qigong want to develop a clearer vision of their purpose in life, as well as reducing their anxiety and finding greater awareness of the world around them and their place in it. The controlled movements are slow and are particularly useful in working with the elderly and those who engage in rigorous sports. The activities are meant to ease tension in the body and develop stability. Qigong opens up the meridians that have been blocked in the body by stress, poor health, injury, or anything else that the body deems as traumatic. These are the routes that the qi needs open so that it can flow freely through them. This openness will make room for the unimpeded movement of energy throughout your body. The philosophy behind qigong is that disease and illness are caused by your life being blocked. When you open up these passages, then you will be able to open the meridians to allow healing energy to flow through when you are sick, or even to prevent the disease from developing.

Reflexology – The focus of the ancients in the east to balance the flow of qi led to the development of reflexology. This practice targets the feet, ears, and hands primarily. It is believed that different systems in your body have a direct connection to other spots on your hands and feet. These can be detoxed and influenced positively to open up the meridians that make those direct connections. Reflexology opens up your energy blockages by encouraging the flow of lymph through relaxation of the muscles and stimulation of pressure points. This manipulation is done with an intense massage that is targeted at a specific area. This method of realigning your life force is thought to increase the circulation in your body as well as balance your energy, boost your immune system and cleanse your body of built-up toxins. The immediate physical effects of a session of reflexology might disappear quickly, but the internal results are unseen and will last a much longer time.

Chakra Healing – The Crown Chakra is the top of the seven internal chakras that the Kundalini must pass through on its way to the Crown Chakra. These are the centers of energy in your body. The seven chakras are thought to resemble seven wheels spinning with power since the word chakra means wheel. The location of the individual chakra in your body will determine what endocrine glands it connects to and which part of the nervous system it controls the function of. They are believed to function much like the meridians in the body for allowing energy to flow through. Your seven chakras are located along your spine from the base of your spine up to the top of your head. They function in a synchronized pattern to allow the energy of the Kundalini to flow through your body. The energy in your chakras must all be balanced because it would not work if one chakra were dull, and the next one was over-energized. The chakras can open and close, which helps to control the flow of energy. If you experience anger, sadness, and negativity, your chakras will likely close themselves. You will use intention, meditation, and breathing to be able to open up your chakras to allow the flow of positive energy and eliminate any negative energy that might be there.

Acupuncture – Ancient cultures teach that the meridians are a map of different routes in your body that allow energy to flow freely through your body. These meridians correspond with specific points where the nervous system, endocrine glands, and muscles interconnect with each other. The acupuncturist uses thin needles to pierce some of the more than six hundred points on the human body that will connect directly with body systems and major organs. These connections are made through the meridians and through the vessels that are associated with the meridians and are known as collaterals. In Chinese culture, the people who know these collaterals and meridians are highly revered. It is believed that acupuncture will help improve the function of your organs and relieve pain in your body by releasing particular adrenal hormones that deal with reducing pain and inflammation. Of all of the different forms of eastern medicine, acupuncture is the one that is most often used in conjunction with western medical practices. Even though needles are used in acupuncture it is often highly relaxing and is considered to be virtually painless.

Reiki – This is a more recent method of eastern healing based on five unbreakable principles: be kind to others, work hard, be grateful, do not worry, and do not become angry. The basis of reiki is the idea that the life force that flows through you can heal you and make you more conscious of your health. It is a method of self-discipline and self-improvement. The idea is to take an active role in healing yourself and keeping yourself healthy while you incorporate the healing qualities of energy into your life. Reiki is based on spirituality, but it is not a religious practice. It is based on the concept of the unseen force of life that flows between all people. That life force can be used for beneficial means when it is properly channeled. Practitioners of Reiki will use hand-on methods of healing to realign energy by balancing it in your body and transferring it to where it is needed the most.

Reject Negativity

Whether you chose to believe in them or even acknowledge them, there are negative entities in your world. The worst kinds of them will live in the lower frequencies of your spirituality. Negativity is attracted to specific types of emotional and mental energy, and it is drawn into different forms of thought that are determined by the content that comes from these emotions. Negative entities are usually not able to be seen by the human eye, but they are felt in your subtle body. They will affect your physical body in ways that can drag down your spirits and can make you physically ill. Those who have already experienced the awakening of their Kundalini will be better able to see these negative entities and to resist their powers. When you are awakened, you will be better able to see or perceive the negative entities lurking in your world because you will be better able to access a broader spectrum of hearing subtle frequencies.

Sometimes a negative entity will attach to a particular person because they are on the same frequency, and their thoughts and feelings are compatible. Some will enter your subtle body because of your attitude and the vibration that you are emitting at a particular moment. Others will come in because of the meditation or dream you had or a particular psychic state that you are in. You might pick up a negative entity while you are traveling a different astral plane or having an out-of-body experience. If you frequently indulge in highly negative forms of entertainment, then you will most likely draw in negative entities. You can become the target of negative entities and psychic predators when you have insufficient internal energy or low self-discipline or esteem.

When negative entities attach themselves to you in a dream, they will enter through a dream sequence or a symbolic vision. This dream may feature scenes or people that you do not recognize that are operating in a dream that looks entirely plausible as if it really could happen. An experienced or awakened person would notice the subtle differences in the vision that points to the fact that it is not reality. These encounters can bring in negative energy as a result of the life that is exchanged between the dreamer and the dream, and these can transfer negative entities over to the spiritual body of the dreamer. This will result in contamination of your mind, and your subtle body as your positive energy is pulled back into the origin of the negative entity, to fuel further dreams and future negative entities.

Sometimes you will create your negative entities. These will come from evil or unhealthy intentions, attitudes, behaviors, or actions. You might do nothing more than laugh at a situation that is not appropriate for laughter, and this would be enough to create a malicious entity. Your thoughts have the power and the ability to manifest themselves as thought forms, and these will be either positive thoughts or negative thoughts, depending on the particular idea that is involved. The intention of the view and the ultimate content will manifest the belief in the spiritual world.

Those negative energies that have already been created will wait around in places of low power for a person who is down on energy to come near. They will then attach themselves to that person. These negative entities will first enter the aura that surrounds the person, their auric field. If they find the opportunity, they will enter the subtle body through holes in the person's aura, primarily if the negative energy and the person are operating on the same frequency. Malicious entities can enter one person through close physical contact with another person. Most people are entirely unaware that this is happening until the happening is over, and the negative entity has attached to them and is affecting their thoughts and feelings.

By expelling the negative entities, you will be able to banish the negativity from your life, which is vital to do when you are attempting to awaken your Kundalini. When you realize a malicious entity has taken over, you can create positive thoughts to drive it away. Negative and positive can't live together in the same space, so the positivity will eventually overcome the negativity. Keeping the negative entities inside will only serve to contaminate your mind and your subtle body. But ridding yourself of negative entities is not always as simple, rejecting the negative things in your life.

Because you may believe that Buddha or Jesus never had any negative thoughts, you may think that you should not have any either. But this is not possible, because you are human and you have the ideas of a human. If you knock yourself down whenever you have a negative thought, then you will merely be judging yourself in ways you should not be judging yourself.

You have negative thoughts, and these negative thoughts carry negative energy. They do bring negative energy, but that energy will only go as far as you allow it to go. If you continuously strive not to have negative thoughts, you will only have more of them. It is like trying not to eat junk food – the more that you think about not eating junk food, the more you are thinking about junk food and wanting to eat it. So when you have a negative thought, feel its energy and then let it go. The secret is not to act on negative thinking because working on it will give it a life of its own. The goal of the inner growth needed to awaken your Kundalini is not to become an entirely positive person but to realize that you are free to think and feel on your own, no matter what the circumstances are around you. When you know that you are free to think as lively or as unfavorable as you want to feel, then the negative entities will no longer hold any power over you because they will no longer interest you. Then the real you can shine positively forward.

Access Your Central Channel

When your Kundalini first awakens, you will feel it somewhere in the region of your tailbone, and you might feel a tingling sensation as it begins to creep up your spine. Awakening Kundalini is quite different from just awakening your energy because the first few times the Kundalini travels up your spine, it may feel something like a small volcano has erupted inside of you. Kundalini will work its way up the center of your spine until it encounters some sort of blockage. It will typically find some type of significant blockage in one of the lower three chakras.

Your Kundalini is highly intelligent, and it will continue to work its way through cycles. It will travel back to the first chakra, the Root Chakra, and then back to its point of origin until it can pass through the Root Chakra unimpeded. It will continue to go through these cycles of dormancy and activity until it can rise through all of the lower six chakras. The effort you put into awakening your Kundalini will be reflected in the power of the Kundalini as it is awakening. If you put more effort into it, then it will be able to open the blocked chakras faster and more efficiently. However, you will feel the effects of this in the release of stored emotions that may cause spiritual, emotional, and physical pain.

When the Kundalini energy has reached the Crown Chakra and unblocked it, then it will have achieved its ultimate goal, and it will be fully awake. When the Kundalini first begins awakening, it is coiled into a tight knot at the base of your spine. When it is fully uncoiled, it will rise out of the Crown Chakra, and you might feel the explosion of energy in your head. You will experience a host of spiritual, mental, and physical changes that might make you feel as though someone or something close to you has died. If you think about it, there has been death for you. It is the death of the way you saw yourself before the awakening and all of the impressions you held about yourself.

The Kundalini will continue to arise through your central channel that is now open and receptive to healing energy. You may feel an intense rush or a gentle wave; the feeling will differ according to what is needed at that moment. Kundalini is a conscious form of energy that is unique to the current situation. You might need to experience another massive rush of energy that flows through your central channel and clears out large amounts of leftover material that is stuck there. You might need the Kundalini to hang out in your Root Chakra, building the vital force that is required to provide the foundation for your physical and subtle body. Whenever the Kundalini is needed longer in any one chakra, it will simmer there as long as it is required to.

Once Kundalini has completed its flow to the Crown Chakra, it will then flow into the primary channels of the body. It will then begin to flow to all of your cells, tissues, and organs. This flow will help to give every part of your body a sense that it is vibrating and glowing. Then the central column will develop if it hasn't already. You will feel that there is a column of energy that extends from the ground underneath your feet up into the air above the top of your head. At first, this will be nothing more than a small column, but it will eventually widen to encompass your entire aura, surrounding your body and your auric field.

When your central channel is open, and you can experience the chakras above and below you, then you will be more connected to your essential nature. You will then be able to realize all components of your humanity and enjoy every part of yourself. This empathy will include all of your thoughts and emotions. Sometimes people will stop before they reach this stage because they are afraid of the openness they feel when their Kundalini is completely awakened and energized. Awakening your upper and lower chakras will allow you to explore deeply your inner chakras, especially the lower ones, and find comfort in your emotional and primal drives.

Visualization

You can use visualization of the Kundalini awakening as a method for bringing life to your Kundalini and letting energy flow freely through your subtle body. The best way to do this is to guide yourself through a practice of meditation that will awaken your Kundalini.

You will begin by sitting comfortably somewhere that you can be quiet, and you will not be disturbed. If you are disturbed during your meditation, it will not work as well, or at all, and you will be left feeling frustrated. It can be difficult enough to practice meditation without any disturbances, so set the scene for you to be successful. Make sure that your environment is ideal for you to relax in. It should be quiet and peaceful, you should be comfortable, and you need to be able to relax your mind and body completely.

Straighten your spine so that you are upright but not rigid. Let your stomach relax and close your eyes entirely but not tightly. Set the focus of your attention on your breathing. Let your breathing naturally slow, which might take a few minutes to accomplish. You want to breathe in and out evenly and deeply as soon as your breathing is deep and regular, set the focus of your attention on your spine. Your spine should be straight. Let your focus travel down your spine until your thoughts rest on the area at the base of your spine. Visualize the bottom of your spine, and begin to see yourself breathing from the base of your spine. As you exhale and inhale, see in your mind that your breaths are coming from the area at the bottom of your spine. Continue your breathing in this manner for a few minutes to establish that your breath is coming from there.

Once you feel that your focus is concentrated enough, see in your mind's eye a small black cylinder with the top removed, and the cylinder is resting at the base of your spine. Visualize a little red baby snake coming out of this cylinder, waving its head from side to side as it explores its surroundings. The baby snake opens its mouth and looks upward toward the top of your spine, hissing while it is investigating. As the baby snake rises along with your spine, picture that its mouth is as large as your entire body, as though it could swallow you whole if it wanted to. As the body rises, the tail will remain near the bottom of the spine. Continue your meditation while you imagine this. During this time, the serpent will often rise and fall back, growing a bit farther with every effort. You will know that your meditation has been successful when you feel enormous feelings of peace and serenity, or when you feel an explosion of energy rising along your spine.

This meditation uses many of the critical aspects of methods for awakening the Kundalini. Doing the meditation will allow you to develop your power of visualization and your powers of concentration. As your awareness becomes more defined, you will become more aware of your chakras and their management. You will also develop the ability to control your breathing and to incorporate your breathing techniques into other areas of your body. You will be able to cleanse your chakras and your channels.

Sometimes when you practice meditation, you will not feel the effects immediately, and you will probably not be successful in the beginning. As you continue to meditate, your chakras and channels will become even more evident each time so that eventually all blockages have been pushed away, and your subtle body is free to be filled with healing energy.

Breathing and Good Posture

People who are just beginning on their practice of meditation often get sidetracked by the idea of breathing. It is normal to wonder if there is a right way to breathe while you are meditating. Most of the meditation experts will recommend that you just let your body breathe naturally. The best way for you to breathe while you are contemplating is for you to breathe the way you usually breathe. If you can push yourself to breathe a bit more deeply, to be able to fill your lungs with more air and your body with more energy, then do so, just don't worry if you can't do it in the beginning. Meditation is not a goal that you need to reach, it is a practice, and you should practice as often as possible.

Part of practicing meditation is to learn to practice mindfulness, and this includes being mindful of your breathing. In your daily life, it is too easy to get caught up in thinking of all of the tasks that are waiting for you to do. When you meditate, you should only be thinking of yourself and your meditation. Following this rule will empty your mind of the stress, anxiety, and distraction that everyday life brings to you.

When you practice mindful breathing during meditation, you will need to pay close attention to your exhalations and inhalations. As you breathe, you will feel different sensations flowing through your body, and you should let your mind enjoy these sensations. See how your chest and your tummy move as you breathe. If they should begin to wander away, bring your thoughts back to your breath. It is usual for your mind to stray, but when you get it back, you are practicing mindfulness. If you can do this for just fifteen minutes every day, you will begin to notice a radical change in how you feel. The simple act of meditation will significantly improve your quality of life. When your mind has learned contentment from meditation, you will have a more positive perception of the world. You will also make better decisions and find more in life to appreciate.

No matter what form your meditation takes, the benefits that you reap will be numerous and unquestionable. When your thoughts are calm, you will be more peaceful, and you will feel happier. It will take time for you to feel the more profound benefits of your meditation, but those benefits will come with time. When you are just beginning, you should only commit yourself to a short period of reflection, like five or ten minutes daily. This is a manageable amount of time for anyone to commit to, and it will get you into the regular daily practice of meditation.

When you have settled yourself into your meditation position, set your focus on your breath as you exhale and inhale. Don't spend any time trying to modify or time your breathing, but just let your breath go in and out in its natural rhythm. You will do your best when you relax and concentrate on one breath coming at a time. If thoughts distract you, acknowledge them and then return directly to your breathing. In the beginning, it can be conducive if you count breath cycles. Begin at the end of an exhalation and calculate the next inhalation and exhalation as one breath cycle. Count the cycles one by one until you reach ten cycles, and then begin again at one. Your goal is not to improve your counting or to try and see how high of a number you can reach. Your goal is to teach you and encourage you to be mindful of your breathing.

After you have spent some time counting your breaths, then enjoy the breathing itself. Watch your chest as it contracts and expands with the air going in and out. Feel your lungs expand and contract. If you practice your breathing techniques regularly and become more mindful of your breathing, then your meditation will deepen and improve with time.

Good posture is essential for good meditation. You do not need to sit on the floor and contort your body into impossible positions. Sit wherever you are most comfortable, and unless you are already a master at yoga positions that will probably be in a chair, or at least on a cushion if you choose to sit on the floor. If you decide to sit in a chair, try not to sit with your back relaxing against the end of the chair, because this position will encourage too much relaxation. It is best to sit more upright, setting a large pillow or a cushion behind your back if needed. Part of meditation is in the body, and if your body is not awake and alert, your meditation will be sluggish and unproductive. Following the basic guidelines for the position of your body that will help you be properly seated and aligned. You should either close your eyes or focus your gaze on a point about six feet in front of you. To keep your cervical spine in alignment, you should keep your chin tucked in slightly. Let your spine follow its natural path, and if it curves a bit, that is okay. Keep your bottom, your sitting bones, stable and centered under your body. Let your palms rest gently on your thighs as your arms are relaxed beside your body. If you cross your legs, keep them loose, with your knees below your hips.

To achieve the primary seated position for meditation, just follow these guidelines. Your body will tense up if your seat is not comfortable, and this will make your meditation difficult. Put your bottom directly in the center of the chair or cushion where you are sitting. Rock back and forth on your bottom when you first sit down, as this will loosen up your sitting bones and allow them to find stable ground for sitting. Once the sitting bones are comfortable, the remainder of your posture will fall into place easily. If your spine is slouched or arched during meditation, your body will fall out of alignment. This will cause your body to strain and feel stiff, and then your mind will find it difficult to concentrate. When you sit down, let your body drape forward at first, and then slowly straighten your spine after your sitting bones are settled. This lets all of your vertebrae in your spine stack on top of each other as you straighten up. You will feel strain in your neck, back, and hips if you sit with your knees above your thighs, so make sure you are sitting where your bottom is above the level of your knees. This might mean that your meditation will be done with you sitting in a chair, and there is nothing wrong with that.

Because your mind tends to be more alert when you are sitting up, it is recommended that you do not meditate while you are lying down. But this is simply a recommendation. If you have any reason that makes sitting uncomfortable, then feel free to do your meditation while you are lying down. Just try to lie flat on your back so that your breathing will be as open as possible.

The point of practicing meditation is to learn to bring the quality of mindfulness into your daily life. Most people spend too much time locked in an office, curved over in front of a computer or a desk. Meditation will allow you to realign your body and bring peace and relaxation into your life.

Once you have awakened your Kundalini, you will experience such a difference in your everyday life. You will find life is no longer mundane as you begin to enjoy the beauty of it every day. You will soon feel a level of energy like you have never known before. And you will feel so free!

CHAPTER 3

Accessing Kundalini Through Open Chakras

The seven internal chakras that lie along your spine are the confined pools of energy that govern your physical health and psychological qualities. The three lower chakras govern your instinctual thoughts and feelings, and the four upper chakras govern your mental and spiritual properties. You need all seven of the chakras to be functioning on the same level of energy so that they will contribute equally to your health and well-being. Your thoughts and feelings need to join forces with your instincts to create the whole you. You can't achieve true inner peace and feel real energy until all of your seven chakras are correctly balanced. The Kundalini will flow through the seven chakras to bring life to the entire body, so all seven chakras must be open to allow the energy of the Kundalini to flow through freely. Since each chakra is individual and separate from the other six, even though they depend on each other and they work together, each chakra will require unique activities to open it and keep it healthy.

The Root Chakra

The foundation of your seven internal chakras is your Root Chakra. It is the body's foundation for overall well-being and good health. You will feel stability, trust, relaxation, security, and prosperity when this chakra is open and healthy. You will think clearly in all areas of your life as well as enjoying plenty of energy. Feeling prepared for the complications of life, as well as feeling centered and calm, are all characteristics that mean that your Root Chakra is open and healthy. You will be mentally and physically at ease with yourself, as well as possessing a great deal of common sense.

When your Root Chakra is not healthy, you will suffer from physical disorders of your lower body. You might suffer from constipation and diarrhea. You can also suffer from anxiety, eating disorders, aches and pains in random places in your body, and chronic illnesses. You will be hampered by feelings of aggression, vulnerability, insecurity, paranoia, and a general inability to truly relax. You might feel that your life is a constant struggle to succeed and that you never really achieve any of the goals that you set for yourself. There are many different ways that you can heal the Root Chakra.

Since red is the corresponding color of the Root Chakra, you will want to focus on incorporating this color into your life as much as possible. When you are meditating, try to imagine a red pool of warm liquid spreading around the base of your spine and covering your Root Chakra in its warmth. Imagine this pool spreading to protect your Root Chakra and the area that surrounds it. Meditate with red cloths covering your area or red candles lit nearby. The Root Chakra also likes the scents with earthy essences like patchouli, sandalwood, and frankincense, so burn these scents as often as possible as incense or with using essential oils in an oil burner. Your Root Chakra also prefers foods that are in the red color family, and it also likes any root vegetable. Fill your diet with beets, onions, carrots, apples, and cherries. Use the gemstones that are red or black to decorate your home and garden, like red jasper, garnet, red carnelian, bloodstone, jet, smoky quartz, and hematite.

You will want to engage in any physical activity that uses the lower body to heal the Root Chakra, particularly standing yoga poses and any dancing. Go for a walk and feel all of the energy from nature seeping up into your legs. If you can walk on grass or sand in your bare feet, then that is even better.

Write down in a journal the things you are doing to heal your Root Chakra, especially the ones that are helping you. Keep note of the things that you need in your life so that you will feel well supported, and also note the items that are supporting you. Think about your roots and how strong they can be, especially ties to your family, friends, and the community. Write down your dreams and goals, and make note whenever you are successful.

When you have opened and healed your Root Chakra, you will then have a strong foundation for your health. This will also provide you with a strong foundation for your other chakras, and it will help you open and heal them. As your Root Chakra grows in strength you will feel more confident and energetic, and you will no longer be driven by guilt and fear. You will then be driven by the knowledge that your life will be just fine, and it will work out the way you want it to be.

The Sacral Chakra

This is the internal center of your creative, emotional, and sexual energy. The physical sensations in your body, as well as your feelings, thoughts, and actions, will let you know when your Sacral Chakra is healthy and when it needs healing. If it needs healing, then you will probably have illnesses or disorders of your lower back, kidneys, and your stomach. Your creativity will be stagnant, and you will overthink everything. You will feed on the drama that others bring to you, and you will either be overly sensitive or overly aloof. Exhaustion will regularly overwhelm you because you will have no energy, and you will likely suffer from sexual tensions and reproductive problems. You will be overly emotional or utterly lacking appropriate emotions. Feeling that you are deprived of any real pleasure in your life will cause you to seek pleasure anywhere that you can find it, which will likely mean that you will be addicted to work, gambling, compulsive shopping, drugs, food, drink, or sexual activity.

A healthy Sacral Chakra will leave you feeling pleased with yourself and comfortable in your skin. You will enjoy being a sexual creature in ways that are healthy for you and well-balanced. Life will not need to be excessive to bring pleasure to you. You will find it easy to be emotionally open with others while remaining emotionally grounded. You will find great joy in the small things in life once again, and your levels of creativity will soar. There are many good ways to heal your Sacral Chakra.

Look into trying new activities and ideas to spur your creativity. Try sewing, quilting, sculpting, drawing, painting, gardening, and photography, cooking, or making jewelry. The idea is to try anything that will light a spark of creativity in your mind and soul. If you find something that you enjoy doing, then take the time to pursue it, since many creative endeavors will take time to learn how to do them correctly. Review all of the ideas about sexuality that you knew when you were a child, and only keep the ones that suit your particular lifestyle. You do not need to live with the ideas and concepts that you learned when you were a child. Ideas about sexuality that do not make you happy will block your Sacral Chakra since it is the chakra that controls your sexuality and your sexual activity.

People will chase pleasure in meaningless or dangerous activities because they have holes in their lives, and they are seeking something to fill them. You might not even realize what it is that you are missing; you just know that something is not right in your life. This pursuit is how people fall into the habits that become addictions. This occasion is where you will need to spend some quality time getting to know yourself. Take the time to remember what was going on in your life when you fell into the addiction. Learn what your emotional triggers are.

Surround yourself with anything orange in color. Wear garments that are orange, or use orange rugs and throws as accent pieces around your house. Eat more of the foods that are orange in color like peaches, papaya, mangos, apricots, sweet potatoes, carrots, and oranges. Even the simple act of setting a bowl full of tangerines, nectarines, and oranges on your kitchen counter or dining room table will make you feel better.

You will also need to embrace the look that your body now has and stop hating it or putting it down. Change your physical appearance if you are not happy with it, but you need to be able to accept that you are working with the way you look right now. Use guided meditations, mostly to reaffirm your love for yourself. Drink some ginger tea or add more ginger to your foods. Do yoga poses that require bending and stretching or take an exercise class. Use essential oils in the fragrances that your Sacral Chakra will love, like orange, neroli, jasmine, ginger, bergamot, or rosewood. Get spontaneous and do things you would not normally do. Pay attention to what makes you feel good and then do more of those activities.

The Solar Plexus Chakra

This one is the third of the lower chakras. You will feel a tremendous inner drive and more self-control and self-confidence when your Solar Plexus Chakra is open and healthy. This chakra can become blocked by traumatic experiences that you have suffered, as well as from bad habits and stubborn mindsets. Some incidents might not seem traumatic to you, but your Solar Plexus Chakra feels that they were. If you were bullied as a child by other children, if your parents were strict authoritarian figures, or if you lived in any situation where the authorities were stringent, then your Solar Plexus Chakra is probably damaged. If you had ever suffered from mental, sexual, emotional, or physical abuse in your lifetime, mostly when you were a child, then your Solar Plexus Chakra is probably blocked or unhealthy.

Your Solar Plexus Chakra is the very center of your willpower and your self-esteem. It needs to be functioning well if you are to be performing well. All of the internal energy that is associated with your actions, intentions, identity, and vitality are directly regulated by your Solar Plexus Chakra. If you need to open or heal this chakra, then you will most likely carry a lot of excess weight around the middle of your body. You can also have diabetes, ulcers, irritable bowel syndrome, and hypoglycemia. You will almost always feel significant fatigue, and you will still be too hot or too cold. Since you will have difficulty forming personal boundaries, then most of your relationships will probably be built on codependency. You will either bully other people or try to dominate others because of your inflated ego, or you will always seek approval from other people because you will suffer from low or no self esteem. You might be addicted to one or more substances because you are either manipulative or weak and powerless.

You will live a harmonious life full of self-confidence when your Solar Plexus Chakra is open and healthy. You will trust in your abilities, and you will be quite comfortable in your skin. You will understand the power that you possess, and you will be satisfied with using it correctly. You will create healthy boundaries for yourself because you will feel more assured in your worth. You will no longer have episodes of explosive anger or times when you minimize yourself because you will respect yourself and other people. You will lose your lethargy and your tendencies toward addiction because you will once again have the energy to drive your performance. You will be energized, focused, empowered, and ready to achieve your goals and seek your dreams.

Essential oils can be used to help open and heal your Solar Plexus Chakra, especially cinnamon, black pepper, rosemary, clove, sandalwood, and cypress. Put several drops of one of these diluted essential oils on your wrists; wear a pendant diffuser as a lovely piece of jewelry, or put some oil into an oil burner and set it near you. You can carry individual crystals with you or wear them, like the tiger's eye, topaz, amber, citrine, and yellow calcite. Certain herbs like lemongrass, rosemary, or chamomile are excellent for opening and healing your Solar Plexus Chakra. You need to focus your diet on essential foods like lentils, spelt, oats, rye, beans, chickpeas, and rice, while using spices such as turmeric, ginger, cumin, and cinnamon.

You will also want to stay away from people who are overly judgmental or overly critical. If you are not able to completely cut ties with them, then limit your contact with them. Spend time with the kind of people who will help to support you and build you up. They will help you find your power and also help you to use it in the right way. Get out of your dull routine and try something new now and then, to add a little emotional spice to your life. You will find renewed levels of energy and get a boost of vitality if you even change one thing in your routine or change one or two of the people in your inner circle that are keeping you down.

You are no longer the victim that you once were. Now is the time to spend some quality time dedicated to learning who you are and what you want out of life. You are no longer powerless and defenseless. You will also no longer sacrifice your desires to make other people happy, just as you will no longer blame your actions on other people. You do not need to be rude just to refuse the ideas of others, but do it politely and go on. Pay attention to what makes you happy spiritually, mentally, and emotionally, and then do those things to take care of yourself, and your Solar plexus Chakra will take care of you.

The Heart Chakra

This is the chakra that is in the center of your physical body, it is the center chakra of the seven internal chakras, and it is also the spiritual and emotional center of your unity, balance, and love. You will feel open and connected to other people when your Heart Chakra is open and healthy. You will also feel receptive, accepting, forgiving, and generous. If your Heart Chakra is closed or unhealthy, then you will likely feel loneliness, resentment, bitterness, fear, and social isolation. Your Heart Chakra will suffer because of many different things. This chakra might need healing if you were raised by or are surrounded by people who are cold and unfeeling. If you have ever suffered from emotional or physical abuse, or if you were denied affection and love as a child, then your Heart Chakra will most likely need healing. And if you harbor unhealthy attitudes and beliefs about the way that love should be or if you have habits that are self-destructive, then your Heart Chakra is probably suffering.

Your Heart Chakra is responsible for regulating the energy in your subtle body that is associated with self-acceptance, compassion, self-love, openness, and the love that you feel for other people. It is the center of your love and emotional balance and the guide to your connections and interactions with other people. When this chakra is healthy, it is open to receiving and giving love, as well as being cleansed, clear, and supportive of your ideals. When the Heart Chakra is unhealthy or blocked, you might suffer from illnesses in your chest with your heart or lungs, or you might suffer from diseases that are connected to these two organs like asthma, high blood pressure, and poor circulation. You will be suspicious of other people, and you will not trust their motives when it comes to your well-being. You will struggle to feel and give real love, so your relationships will most likely be built on codependency. You will continuously replay in your mind any trauma you have suffered in your life, and this might make you needy, anxious, fearful, and self-critical. Bitter thoughts and feelings will sometimes overwhelm you, and you will find it difficult to let go of them. Your style of love will swing wildly between being emotionally distant in your relationships and being utterly terrified of being alone.

The Heart Chakra loves the color green, so try to surround yourself with this color, especially if it takes you out into nature. Fill your home with as many houseplants as you can, and grow a garden if you have space. Use herbs like astragalus, rose, hawthorn, holy basil, nettle, and angelica to make sachets for your room or to carry with you. Use the heart healing crystals of jade, rose quartz, ruby, green fluorite, emerald, and malachite as jewelry for your person or as decoration in your home. Rose, marjoram, lavender, neroli, and angelica essential oil can be worn on the skin or burned in a burner for scented oil to give off the scents. Try to add more green heart-healing foods into your diet. Your Heart Chakra will love zucchini, spinach, kale, cabbage, kiwis, avocados, peas, broccoli, green apples, pears, Swiss chard, grapes, celery, and lettuce. And the yoga poses that are meant for healing, like the camel pose, fish pose, cobra pose, or the forward bend, are especially helpful.

Meditation will help to heal your Heart Chakra, especially meditation that is based on loving affirmations for yourself. Set personal boundaries and personal limits, because you don't need to be agreeable to all people all of the time. Count your blessings, and never take love and life for granted. It will be difficult for you to show love to others if you do not love yourself or if your mind is overly critical. Think of what other people might be going through, so that you don't take their actions personally all of the time. Embrace your own emotions, because there is nothing wrong with occasionally feeling bored, sad, unhappy, angry, or jealous, as long as you do not allow yourself to dwell on those feelings for too long. Allow yourself to give love to other people and receive love from them, and learn to accept compliments graciously.

The Throat Chakra

You will be able to be creative, honest, confidant, assertive, and not afraid to speak your truth when your Throat Chakra is balanced. When it is blocked or unhealthy, then you will have problems with dishonesty, stubbornness, social anxiety, and shyness, lack of trust in others, verbal aggressiveness, and a deep fear of expressing your inner feelings and thoughts out loud. When children are forbidden to express themselves in any usual way like verbally or creatively, if they are continuously criticized by the figures of authority in their lives, or if they are constantly belittled and made to feel worthless, then they will probably grow into people who have a blocked or unhealthy Throat Chakra. This chakra holds the energy that regulates your authenticity, creativity, and understanding.

When your Throat Chakra is blocked or unhealthy, then you might experience sinus infections, respiratory infections, or infections of the throat. You might suffer from hyperthyroidism or hypothyroidism, or your lymph nodes might be swollen continuously. Your voice might often break or sound nasally or thin, and you might have premature hearing loss or ear infections. You find honesty something that is too hard for you to subscribe to regularly, often doing one thing and saying something else. Your partner makes most or all of the decisions in your relationships since you are quiet and trying to keep the peace. You are either painfully shy or overly opinionated. Being misunderstood and suffering from miscommunications is no stranger to you.

You will want to begin to heal your Throat Chakra with meditations that focus on thoughts of love and acceptance of yourself as well as words that allow you to think or feel. Write your deepest, most private thoughts in a journal so that you will be in the regular habit of expressing your inner feelings. Surround yourself with things that are colored blue since this is the color of the Throat Chakra. Add more blue foods into your diet like grapes, currants, blueberries, blackberries, and plums. The Throat Chakra also likes peaches, lemons, grapefruit, apples, kiwis, lemons, pears, figs, and apricots. Use herbs to heal the Throat Chakra, like elderberry, spearmint, cinnamon, echinacea, fennel, and cloves, making any of these into a soothing tea, either by themselves or in combinations. Blue crystals that you can wear or carry include tanzanite, larimar, blue kyanite, azurite, aquamarine, and lapis lazuli. Always drink pure water and use the essential oils eucalyptus, frankincense, neroli, clove, rosemary, and myrrh.

Release the energy that might be built up in your physical throat by laughing, screaming, or singing. Tune-up the voice of your subtle body by sitting in silence, especially under a clear blue sky or near a body of water. Try to practice being more assertive when you are alone. Try to speak kindly, but forcefully, when dealing with other people.

The Third Eye Chakra

All of the energy that is associated with your perceptions, thoughts, realities, and intuitions are centered in your Third Eye Chakra. A doorway to divine spiritual enlightenment is opened when your Third Eye Chakra is open and healthy. You will possess strong intuition, clarity, insight, self-awareness, and emotional balance when your Third Eye Chakra is open and healthy. If this chakra is closed or unhealthy, then you will most likely suffer from paranoia, anxiety, cynicism, mental illnesses, depression, and mood swings, and disorders. If you were a child who was taught never to question authority, or anything else, then your Third Eye chakra is probably blocked or unhealthy.

Physically this chakra controls your face and its parts, so when it is blocked or unhealthy, then you will probably suffer from earaches, problems with your vision, migraines, and sinus issues. Your temperament will either be arrogant and opinionated or dreamy and ungrounded. You will find it difficult to be open-minded because your stubbornness will regularly get in your way. Since you usually mistrust other people or automatically dislike them, the bulk of your relationships and interactions with other people will be trivial and superficial. You will have rigid ideas about how the world should be run and how people should behave. You will find it difficult to connect to your deeper self or your soul because you will not view reality as clearly as you need to to be open with yourself. You might also find yourself to be addicted to anything that will bring you feelings of pleasure.

If you genuinely want to open this chakra and make it healthy, then you will need to be willing to seek out and explore new and different points of view. This will help you break the pattern of being rigid and close-minded in your thoughts and beliefs. You will also need to practice grounding yourself, in reality, to avoid being lost in fantasy and delusion. Don't let your mind wander too often, as you need to practice mindfulness and keep yourself grounded in the present. Healing the Third Eye Chakra will require quite a lot of soul-searching and soul growth, and this will help you to feel more compassion for other people. You will also find it easier to reach your mystical state of being.

Spending time in bright sunlight will help you clear your mind and heal your Third Eye Chakra. When you are cooking, try to use herbs like saffron, basil, star anise, mugwort, jasmine, lavender, rosemary, lotus, or passionflower, or use them to burn as incense. You can also make delicious teas out of any of these herbs. Purple is the color of the Third Eye Chakra, so try adding more purple foods to your diets like blackberries, prunes, dates, raisins, figs, purple cabbage, blueberries, purple kale, and purple carrots. The essential oils that are appropriate for healing this chakra are frankincense, patchouli, sandalwood, juniper, vetiver, and clary sage. And you will want to carry or wear crystals of sapphire, shungite, lapis lazuli, amethyst, and kyanite. Standing forward bend and child's pose are the right yoga positions for healing this chakra.

The Third Eye Chakra will be damaged if you continuously hold onto core beliefs that limit your thinking. These are the deep convictions that you have about your fears, insecurities, and self-esteem. You will never be able to fully open and heal the Third Eye Chakra if you can't uncover the self-limiting beliefs that you are holding on to. You must be more self-aware if you want to heal this chakra. When you continue to identify with specific thoughts or feelings just because you have always held them, without really understanding why then you will find it impossible to heal this chakra. You need an open and healthy Third Eye Chakra to help you interpret your dreams and to reach out to other realms of possibility. And always tell yourself how well you are doing, especially when you can use phrases that describe how you see or create.

The Crown Chakra

This chakra is the uppermost of the seven internal chakras and the ultimate goal of the Kundalini. On a cosmic level, it is the energy center of your conscious thought. This chakra will connect you to the divine because it is the location of your real awareness. You will connect more quickly to your higher self when the Crown Chakra is open and healthy. You will tap into your inner wisdom, feel connected to other people and all of nature, see the larger picture more efficiently and feel an overwhelming sense of serenity and wholeness. If the environment that you are living in is full of trauma and stress, your Crown Chakra will most likely be blocked or unhealthy.

When this happens, you will probably suffer from neurological disorders or chronic illnesses of the endocrine system. You might be ultra-sensitive to bright light or suffer from migraines. You can experience delusions, insomnia, nightmares, night terrors, fog and mental confusion, and chronic fatigue. You will be a person who is very rigid in their thoughts and is materialistic, greedy, lonely, and spiritually disconnected. You will prefer to be isolated from other people, and your ego will likely be out of control because you don't feel any real care or compassion for other people.

Your access to enlightenment and the window to your soul is your Crown Chakra. When this chakra is open and healthy, then you will feel more inner peace and clarity as well as feeling more enlightened in your thoughts and feelings. You will feel a fantastic feeling of connection to all of humanity that will replace your former sense of isolation. You will finally belong to the universe. Life will once again be a beautiful thing since you will no longer be bored with it. You will live in the moment, and your reality will be defined by expansiveness and spontaneity.

Meditation is one of the fastest and easiest ways that you can heal your Crown Chakra. Spend some time allowing your thoughts to flow freely without trying to guide them. Watch movies and read books that you might not usually enjoy to broaden your horizons. Examine your feelings for those that deal with ignorance or prejudice, and get rid of them. You will spend less time on the thoughts and feelings that limit you when you enjoy more time with other people and trying to learn about other people.

You need to simplify your life by decluttering your immediate surroundings. An excess of belongings creates mess and clutter that will eventually lead to mental and emotional distress. You will be purifying yourself when you cleanse and simplify your environment. It is also essential while you are washing the physical space that you set aside a space for your daily meditations. These are vital for the health of your Crown Chakra. Put meaningful things in your meditation space, things like crystals, books, candles, or incense. Your spiritual practice might be unique to you, so you might want to write or read, pray or meditate, or sing or practice yoga or meditation.

You will want to spend time every day looking for signs from the divine signs that you are being communicated with by a higher power. Be open to the guidance that is coming from this source. This will help to open and heal your Crown Chakra so the Kundalini will have a receptive chakra to go to when it awakens inside you.

Kundalini and the Chakras

When the Kundalini awakens, it creates a free flow of energy that travels up through the chakras to the Crown Chakra, the top chakra of the seven internal chakras. When this energy leaves its dormant state at the base of your spine and travels upward, it creates an awakening that will lead to an expanded state of consciousness. When you open the central channel and open and heal the chakras to give the Kundalini free space to travel, the resulting experience will fill you full of life and energy far beyond any you have ever known.

CHAPTER 4

Signs Your Kundalini Is Awakened

A Kundalini awakening is a specific set of energetic experiences that will resolve all of the issues in your psyche. This experience will lead you to true enlightenment. Awakening your Kundalini will awaken the cosmic energy that is lying dormant inside of you. Once it is revived, it will create a gateway through your Crown Chakra, and it will connect you to an unlimited source of energy radiating from the universe. You can then tap into those energies so that you will be able to live a more full and fantastic life.

Many of the symptoms of a Kundalini awakening will come from changes to your nervous system. This makes it easy to confuse the symptoms of the awakening for some sort of neurological or biological condition you might be having. The symptoms of Kundalini awakening are signs that your body is trying to regain its balance or is trying to increase its levels of energy.

The symptoms of Kundalini awakening will happen all during the process. There will be symptoms during pre-awakening, at the actual spiritual awakening, and after the Kundalini awakening. All of these symptoms will lead you to a complete Kundalini transformation. After each event of a change, your body will produce signs of the physical changes. The interval between the episodes will not matter. Self-realization is not only a biological and spiritual process; it is also a gradual process. Since it is a gradual process, your ability to sustain your quiet mind during these processes will grow over time. Having a quiet and peaceful mind is crucial to gaining a full Kundalini awakening. The longer the period that you can maintain a calm mind, the stronger the symptoms of your Kundalini transformation will be. If you are progressing continuously in your spiritual transformation, then your signs of Kundalini awakening will get closer together each time that you experience them. After the first big rush of awakening, your symptoms will continue non-stop until your transformation is complete, growing gradually stronger every day.

When you are in the pre-awakening stage, you will experience specific types of symptoms. These symptoms are often due to changes that are happening in your mind. You will have insights, vivid dreams, and visions. You can experience many changes in your beliefs of the Universe and your feelings about other people. The world will begin to look like a very different place for you. You might start to question the beliefs in religion that you have held since you were a baby. The growing energy is working inside of your mind to clear out certain aspects of how you see the world and how you see your place in the world. As your mind becomes quieter, your eyes become more open, and you begin to see everything more consciously.

You will feel a sudden rise in energy as your Kundalini begins to open. You will start to see nature differently, with vivid colors instead of flat shades of grey. Your overall perception will change. Time will seem to stand still, and you will be able to see the way everything in the Universe is interconnected easily. You will feel Kundalini awakening symptoms like flashes of light, rushes of energy, and overall warmth. You will now have vivid dreams and visions about things you didn't know before. It will seem as though the information is being downloaded to you from some unknown source. You will begin to receive information about your purpose in life and the lessons you will need for this lifetime. As the energy in your soul begins to blossom, you might be able to recall some of your past lives. There are as many different versions about the symptoms of a Kundalini awakening as there are people who have experienced an awakening because everyone will experience something unique. Your personal feelings and beliefs will profoundly influence your personal experience. One common theme is that everyone is suddenly able to see past their limitations and begin to enjoy the wisdom that comes from a higher power. There is an expanded sense of perception and sensory abilities. These heightened abilities will seem to fade over time, but that just means you have become used to the sensations and are more comfortable with them.

The symptoms you experience toward the end of your Kundalini awakening are mostly combinations of different healing reactions that your body is having. You may experience emotional problems or physical illnesses. It is not uncommon for people to feel unwell in the first days of the Kundalini awakening, but this is nothing more than your body getting rid of the negative energy as the positive energy of the Kundalini moves in.

Just before your Kundalini begins to open, you might feel specific symptoms that will let you know that the transformation is about to happen. These might be as simple as twitching muscles or tingling in the nerves. It might be as unusual as sporadic jerking of your limbs, cramps, pain in various areas of your body, or flashes of light before your eyes. When you feel these things, try not to panic, but take them for the positive signs that they are. When these begin, you will likely be able to hold your meditations for more extended periods and make them deeper. You will feel yourself falling into a state of trance during your meditations that is deeper than you have ever experienced before. You will probably try to fight the feeling because you will feel like you are losing control of your body. In essence, you will be losing control, but it will be to your higher self and not some unknown being that you would need to fear. Let yourself fall into this trance and feel your meditations deepen and strengthen. If you do not think your reflections are trying to deepen like this, it might merely mean that you are still stuck at an early stage of awakening. Everyone will awaken at their rate. You might want to try to convince yourself that you are farther along than you are, but remember to take your time with your awakening.

Because there is so much false information surrounding the Kundalini awakening, you might see that some of the symptoms are described quite colorfully and exaggerated beyond what they are. The majority of your symptoms will be due to changes happening in your central nervous system. When your Kundalini transformation is entirely happening, the symptoms will occur daily, and they will get stronger as you come closer to your full awakening. You will eventually come near the end of your awakening and reach a plateau, and then all of the symptoms you have been feeling will begin to settle down. The only things that won't subside are your awareness level and your vibration, and these will become stronger every day.

Emotional Turmoil

During and after your Kundalini awakening, you will need to be more mindful of your inner feelings and emotions. This might be the most difficult one to put into action. Awakening your Kundalini will require you to recognize and process the negative emotions you have, as well as be able to release them out of your body. Most people have never been taught how to do this. Negative emotions most often remain trapped in your mind, heart, and soul because you have been told it is not safe to deal with those feelings, so they must be kept locked away and never acknowledged. You have activated an unconscious defensive mechanism for keeping those feelings buried. As a child, people may have often told you to 'grow up,' 'stop crying,' or 'suck it up' so many times that you learned not to show those feelings to anyone. Unfortunately, this means not offering them to yourself either.

You internalized all of your negative feelings because you felt that something must be wrong with you for feeling them in the first place. But the only way to truly heal is to learn to feel the full extent of your emotions, and even though this can be challenging, you can teach yourself to unlock all of those buried emotions. Burying your pain and your negative feelings will only result in the development of emotional problems, chronic illnesses and diseases, depression, and various addictions. Your body and your mind are looking for ways to soothe the pain. While none of this is your fault, you will need to be willing to deal with all of it if you are ever going to heal.

Awakening your Kundalini will assist you on this journey since she will be the one to teach you how to dig out your buried emotions and bypass all of your defenses to begin the healing process. This will happen automatically as a by-product of your Kundalini awakening. This will all, unfortunately, begin without your knowledge, and when you realize it is happening, you will need to deal with it and not repress any of your feelings. This is where you will need to consciously accept that change will happen to you, and it will be for the better of you.

You will need to work on reprogramming your reaction to pain and your perception of pain in your body. Your mind has already been programmed to see problems as a type of distress that needs to be avoided. Your conscious mind would prefer to seek out pleasure and relief. This action helps you to be able to recognize when someone has crossed one of your boundaries. Now is the time when you will be forced to deal with the old pains that your Kundalini awakening will bring out. You will need to deal with these old emotions and not try to repress them again, because trying to push them back will only make the energy of the Kundalini fish them out again, and you will be caught up in a vicious cycle of fighting with yourself. Your defenses will naturally be alarmed and on high alert, but if you fight this process, you will be fighting an exhausting battle that you will eventually lose. If you continue to feel that pain is unsafe, and it is wrong for you to feel it, then you will be struggling to win a battle against yourself that will have no positive outcome. You will need to teach your mind that emotional pain means that this part of your life is beginning to heal. You will also need to realize that this is one of the most significant changes you will make on your spiritual journey. Since Kundalini awakening will activate your fight-or-flight response, this is an essential concept for your mind to accept.

You can begin to retrain your brain by making a list of all of the occasions where allowing pain to be what it has resulted in a bit of learning for you. Your mind will probably need some amount of convincing, and this is fine. You will need to try to believe in this idea and not just force your mind to accept it as a fact. You have most likely lived your entire life doing your best to fit in with the expectations you were given, but you will abandon yourself and your potential if you do not accept your emotions and feelings. Kundalini awakening will require you to be yourself and to be honest with yourself so that you can take all of the wounded parts of yourself and love them until they can heal.

So when your Kundalini is awakening, and you have strong negative feelings and emotions rising, you will need to deal with them. You can work on different things to acknowledge your feelings and begin to heal your emotions. You will find that not every emotion or feeling will require a lot of attention, so you will need to work on knowing which ones need you and which ones don't. Some of your emotions will be too intense to address directly. Be patient with yourself because dealing with your feelings instead of burying them is a new skill. You will need to work to practice this to be good. You can do specific things that can emotionally support yourself during your Kundalini awakening.

Start by asking yourself what you are feeling at this particular moment. Try to keep your answer to the question in one word, since this will be easier for you to deal with. Describe your emotion with words like angry, desperate, sad, frustrated, lonely, and so on. You might be feeling several different emotions all at the same time, and this is perfectly normal. Imagine that the Kundalini is a fire, crawling through the underbrush of your feelings. When real fire attacks a forest, all of the little woodland creatures will run away in fear and hide somewhere until the fire is over. The fire will burn off all of the dead brush that is decaying the forest. A Kundalini awakening is much like a fire coursing through your body, getting rid of all the deadly emotions that are rotting your soul. Once you have named all of your thoughts, you can begin to offer help and compassion to your inner child, who is struggling with all of these changes.

Feel the emotion or feeling without actively trying to get rid of it or resolve it. Ask your body where it is most feeling this emotion and then try to relieve the tension that is likely building in that body part. Your intention should be to meet this emotion with compassion, curiosity, and love. Let the feeling know that you don't mean to harm it or try to resolve it, that you want to let it be what it is. If you sit with an emotion or a feeling long enough, it should shift by itself and might even disappear. Either way, it will most likely lose most of its strength or its power to cause you pain. If the emotion doesn't go away on its own, then concentrate on it for a while. Feel it filling your body and breathe deeply and evenly so that your body will continue to be nourished while the emotion tries to take over. Give the feeling a name. Keep feeling it until it loses its power over you.

Try to express the emotion or feeling out loud. Sometimes emotions just want an outlet and a way to know they are being acknowledged. Write about the feeling in a journal or draw a picture of it. Ask the emotion of how it would like to be portrayed. Hold on to the feeling as long as you possibly can without trying to get rid of it. Some emotions will be stronger than what you can deal with in one experience. Anger is one of the most intense emotions and it usually will need more than one incident to rid you of it.

During and after your Kundalini awakening, you will be releasing deep emotions and a strong feeling that you may have kept repressed for many years. This might be very painful for you to do, but it is needed if you are to move along through your transformation to your true enlightenment. This new awakening will require you to leave old emotions and pains behind so that you can continue to grow and develop your unity with the Universe.

Repressed Memories

When a person is experiencing a traumatic event, their conscious mind will often shut itself off so that they are not forced to share the event as it is happening. It is a defense mechanism of the mind to protect the person from the traumatic event. But even though the person has no recollection of the event, their reason is still storing memories of the event in their subconscious. These are known as repressed memories, and they can directly affect you, even if you do not realize that they are causing an effect on your life. Some situations are more common for causing repressed memories like domestic abuse, physical violence, sexual abuse, wartime events, and traumatic injuries you suffer as the result of an accident. No matter what kind of event caused the block in your mind, the suppression of the event is essential to your mind because it will allow you to continue to function as though the event never happened.

Even though you might not remember a repressed event, it is still with you, and it will still affect your daily behavior. These memories will eat at your mind, staying far enough in the background that you are not consciously aware of them. But because those memories have no emotions associated with them since they are repressed, they can't be released from your mind, and you can't be healed of them. They exist, but to you, they don't live. The influence happens on the unconscious level of your mind, but the effect occurs at the conscious level of your mind. Those who were endured sexual abuse as children may overeat as adults because something in their mind is telling them that if they are unattractive, they will be safe from harm. You can't heal the effects of traumatic events until you can acknowledge them and deal with them.

When you experience a Kundalini awakening, everything about your mind and your soul will be open and alive. It will be impossible for you to fully feel the transformation if your mind is not fully open, and when your awakening is complete, your mind will be fully accessible. Your repressed memories will be triggered, and they will once again be opened for your scrutiny. They might not come all at once, because your awakening might not be completed all at once, but they will make themselves known to you. Certain sights, sounds, or odors might invoke an unpleasant reaction. You may have visions in your dreams. Your repressed memories are most likely to be revealed to you in your dreams because your brain likes to work on healing pathways and memories while you are asleep. When you have a vivid imagination, especially about repressed memory, it is just your higher-self beginning to send messages to your lower-self during your Kundalini awakening. There is a story that needs to be told and brought into your conscious thoughts.

You might be tempted to stop your Kundalini awakening at this point simply because unlocking the repressed memories is too painful, and you do not feel strong enough to go on. But don't stop here, because once you get past these memories unlocking, then you will be able to deal with them and get rid of them for good. You will need to trust that you have the power to complete this unlocking process. You have made so much progress at this point. Tell yourself that you are willing to do these things so that you can improve your life. You know that these repressed memories have been holding you back and causing you pain. Your repressed memories limit your abilities to live a full and happy life, and it is time to let them go forever. You don't need your mind to protect you from these memories any longer. Your awakening Kundalini will provide you with the energy that you need to work through this. You will feel pain, both emotionally and physically, while you are working through the repressed emotions and memories. Your Kundalini is opening the door and removing the blocks your conscious mind has erected. Now that you can see what is wrong, you have the power to correct it.

Physical Symptoms

Kundalini awakening has much to do with the changes that your mind and your emotions go through. But your body will also experience physical changes as part of the transformation that may be confusing to you. As long as you do not have any underlying medical conditions, all of these symptoms will be perfectly normal. The energies associated with spiritual awakening can cause some bizarre symptoms.

You might feel activity at the top of your head or pressure in different parts of your head. It can be quite common for you to feel a tingling, an itching, or a buzzing sensation around or in parts of your scalp and skull. The energy of the Kundalini awakening will cause subtle changes in the receptors that you use for downloading and learning information. You might feel a spirit guide communicating with you, but it will be in a different part of your brain than where you usually think sensations of your thoughts.

All levels of your focus may feel extra sensitive. You might begin to hear things at lower or higher frequencies than you did before the awakening. The colors that you see might be more luminous and more vivid than you remember. When you touch things, the feeling will be more intense than before, and the scents you smell may seem to be overpowering. You also might suddenly be able to taste different layers in your food, and tastes you are not used to tasting.

Your body might suddenly begin to have growing pains, those strange pains you might recall from your childhood. You might also feel strange aches, almost like you have the flu, or you might suddenly have a burst of unexplained energy. You might become bloated or have other digestive issues. You might see a change in your intimate desires. All of these symptoms are common reactions to the surge of energy you will feel during a Kundalini awakening.

Your weight might begin to change while you are going through your transformation. If you find yourself needing less food and sleep, then you might lose some weight, or you might gain a little if you find yourself eating and sleeping more. Your body will decide what it needs, and it will expect you to provide for its needs. And you may have strange cravings for different foods. Your body might be trying to tell you that it lacks a particular nutrient. Having a Kundalini awakening is not an excuse to eat everything in sight, but give in to a few of your cravings to soothe your body now and then.

Since you are experiencing a rebalancing on many different levels, you might feel physically dizzy sometimes. Your inner ear is a susceptible organ, and it controls your sense of balance. Feelings of dizziness might also be due to fluctuations in your blood pressure. Your body is also realigning itself, even down to your DNA on the cellular level, so your sense of balance might be a bit off. Be more deliberate in your actions, and try to pay attention to what you are doing in the present moment to help reduce the possibility of sudden falls.

You may be prone to episodes of intense rushes of energy. Your body will be resonating with the new powers of a higher frequency, which is one of the best and most exhilarating of all of the physical symptoms of a Kundalini awakening. The Kundalini needs to rise through the central channel that runs along your spine, which is where your internal chakras are located. As the energy from the Kundalini awakening travels up the central track, it will need to go through these chakras, and if they are blocked, the power will open them wide so that it can proceed. The chakra will be cleared, old memories in your cells will be cleared out, and your body will respond with joyous lightening in the form of a giant rush of energy. Unfortunately, since you are on a spiritual roller coaster ride, your periods of tremendous highs might be followed with periods of devastating lows that leave you feeling exhausted. Rest when you need to and remember that this will eventually pass.

You are now probably nourishing your body in better ways than you used to, and you get further into your transformation. You will be consuming more nutrients, and this will create positive changes in your body. One of the most effortless changes to see is that your hair and nails will probably begin to grow much more quickly than they used to. But along with this positive trend, you may notice some adverse food-related effects of the awakening, usually in the form of food intolerances and allergies you never had before. This might just be your body telling you that a particular food is no longer suitable for you because it does not nourish your new body in the way your body needs.

Humans are not usually fond of change, and they often feel moments of anxiety when things change that are beyond their control. Your Kundalini awakening will not be in your possession. A spiritual awakening will require you and your body to adjust on many different levels. Breathe evenly, deeply, and slowly, and try your best to keep your thoughts in the present when they begin to race and flutter all over the place. Take in the breath and focus on it; be thankful for the oxygen that is flowing into your lungs and filling your body. Remind yourself that these symptoms will pass and that you are entirely safe. You might also feel a bit of fogginess in your left brain. Your right mind is in charge of your creativity and your imagination. All of your intuitive thinking comes from the right side of your brain, that thinking that goes beyond logical thought and any impressions that your five senses might bring to you. The left brain is the analytical side of your mind. It is responsible for rational and linear thinking. Your right brain will surge forward quickly to align itself with the Kundalini awakening. Your left brain will most likely skip and stick because it doesn't quite know what to do in these situations. The feelings and emotions of the Kundalini awakening make no sense to your left brain, so that it might feel a bit foggy at times.

The energy of the Kundalini awakening might alter your sleeping habits. There will likely be nights when you are so full of life that you are unable to fall asleep or stay asleep. Then you will have nights when eight hours is nowhere near the amount of sleep that you need. During this time, you should rest when your body needs to, and try not to be too exhilarated when your body is experiencing a rush of energy. And don't feel bad if you need more sleep than usual. When you are sleeping is the time when your body heals itself from all of the things it has suffered during the day. It will also be more comfortable for your body to dump out the toxins that the Kundalini awakening is releasing if your body is well-rested.

As you move through the awakening experience, you might find periods when the look of your skin changes, especially the skin on your face. The energy that comes with the Kundalini awakening will improve your skin and make you look younger. The stress that you might sometimes feel during this period might make you look older than you are. And with all of the toxins of repressed memories and old intentions being released from your cells, your skin might undergo other changes, like the development of acne or eczema. These symptoms will pass as you work further through your transformation, and your skin will settle down once the toxins are cleansed away, and the energy levels balance out.

Self-Realization

At some point in your Kundalini awakening, you will come to realize that the Divine inspires your life. Your genuine reason for being is the relationship between the human part of you and the Divine part of you. When the boundaries of whatever spirituality or religion that you subscribe to are not enough to hold you any longer, when you begin to feel a hunger for your own spiritual experiences that are personally connected to you, then you have come to your self-realization.

The spiritual awakening you are experiencing is the beginning of your ascent toward really knowing yourself. This will help to emancipate you from the past illusions that have kept your psyche imprisoned in service to your false self. A Kundalini awakening is an emotionally spiritual experience that will take you to spiritual levels you only dreamed of before. You will find yourself trying to get rid of the principles that previously regimented you into submission. You will be like a new baby during your spiritual awakening, and you may feel quite vulnerable. You will not realize your enlightenment by trying to become anything in particular or pursue anything in particular. When you develop the ability to let go and be, it will come to you. You will need to let go of your ego and let your subtle body take control of you.

You will know you are achieving self-realization when you can let go of the fear the holds you tied to familiar things only because they are familiar. You probably have thoughts and emotions that do not serve any purpose to you, but you have hung onto them for so long that they have become a habit that you have kept. You have been kept in mental and emotional darkness by religious ideas and societal mores that were forced upon you. You fear being persecuted if you do not follow them, and you fear the unknown that is beyond the beliefs you subscribe to. But your desire to know true enlightenment is more potent than any fear you may be holding onto, so you take the risk and seek enlightenment and transformation. You found your inner courage and jumped feet first into the possibility that life will be better on the other side.

This journey has left you without any real sense of yourself, without the familiar beliefs and ideas that kept you grounded in your past reality. When you began to let go of your ego, you discovered that all of your boundaries and limits came into question. You are probably now wondering precisely who you are. And your transformation will provide you with many possible answers to that question. Every solution that you receive will send you seeking in a particular direction that may or may not be the way you need to go. And during your travels, your psyche will be struggling to pull you back together so you can be the person you were before the awakening began. If you have not yet started to venture out mentally and spiritually, know that it is coming. It happens to everyone who undergoes a Kundalini awakening. Your psyche chooses to continue to believe what it now believes. It is a rite of passage for you to seek your better self, and it requires new areas where you will need to grow and learn.

You will also find that a wide array of choices is now available to you. This Kundalini awakening will give you new insights into your life and the person you will become. You might feel the need to break new ground in an unfamiliar area. You might decide to become a teacher of the new way of life you will soon be enjoying, and you will spend time studying and learning. You might feel you must fight the old ideas with all the force of a rebel in a new land. You might even find that an alternative identity suits you better than the one you carry now. You can choose to be a shaman, seer, psychic, clairvoyant, or a medium; there will be many spiritual paths open to you and your talents. Be careful of what you decide to chase or take on during this time. Exploring new worlds is a marvelous thing to do, but if you take on a unique personality, it will be just another ego that you will need to get rid of. You will not truly enjoy your spiritual awakening until you can abandon all of your efforts to have a self. You won't need to replace your old self with any sort of new self, no matter how much better you think the new one might be. The truth is that the real you have always been you, and that is enough for the Universe. The Divine powers ask that you simply be you, without trying to wear any sort of mental or spiritual disguise.

Your spiritual awakening is your ability to transition to your next level of awareness, your self-realization. True self-realization will only happen when you can transition past the mistaken idea that you need to have some sort of definition that you need to be defined by a particular persona. You already have an identity, and that is you. You will not know or find your true self in the limits of your thinking mind. If you pursue your true self with the idea that you will merge yourself with it, then you will only succeed in creating another illusion. You are not able to integrate with what you already are. Trying to label yourself or define yourself will stand in the way of your true enlightenment. You are not only your physical body, but you are also not only your emotions, and you are not only your thoughts. You need to learn to let go.

When you have learned to let go of your ego, then your true self will be able to reveal your true nature through your open mind. When you know to stop trying to become someone, when you stop trying to identify with particular things when you stop trying to be someone, then your ego will melt away. These ego structures distort your sense of reality, and they need to be stilled so that your true self can shine through.

Empathic Abilities

Being an empath and this powerful spiritual awakening that you are undergoing are genuinely connected. You might have trouble imagining a time when your thoughts and emotions will be collected, calm, and balanced. You might feel as though you will never again enjoy a level of mental state or feel as though your sanity has returned. Although it may seem to be in the distant future, or maybe it seems impossible right now, it is just another part of this fantastic journey that you are on.

You might sometimes feel burdened by your empathic abilities, but this is just another part of the process of spiritual awakening. When you are an empath, you can understand the feelings and experiences of other people even if you have never personally felt the same feelings or experienced the same experiences. During your spiritual awakening, you will find that your empathy and your emotions are quite sensitive, and there will be some excellent reasons for these feelings.

You might feel that something important has changed inside of you. You might think that something is different, but you can't explain the feeling. You feel like you want to become someone new who has nothing to do with who you were before. You will visualize things in a wholly unique manner because you are looking at the world with a new vision.

You will know that your old life was not desirable, that something in that life was just not right. You understand that the older adult you used to be was lacking in something meaningful. You finally understand all of the things that you used to do in your life but don't want to anymore and all the old patterns you don't want to repeat. Because you are ready for notable changes in your life, you never want to go back to that old life.

You will want to surround yourself with people who feel like you feel now. Not everyone will evolve in their spiritual process at the same rate, and you might find that you will need to leave some people behind as you grow beyond them. This can be a painful experience, but you need to align yourself with the people who are more like the new you. You need to be with people who have a comparable level of energy and enlightenment. You find it easy to connect with them because you are on the same wavelength they are. You are no longer connecting to people on the superficial level of exchanging ideas, but you are now connecting to others with your soul. This kind of connection is not likely to be ruled by your ego.

You are no longer interested in anything superficial. You are seeking the real thing, those things that are authentic in life. You might be feeling that you have become antisocial or complicated, but you also know that it is not healthy if you are easily able to accept things that are less than perfect. Follow the call of your heart, because it will take you where you should be. It is never easy to experience a spiritual awakening. As you become less entranced in your ego and more aware of the world around you, then you will also become acutely aware of the sadness and despair in the world around you. When you see the suffering in the world and understand the disparity more, it can lead you into depression because you can now feel their pain even if you have never experienced their lifestyles. You will also know that attending to your own needs is no longer enough. You will have a deep need to help other people and make a positive impact on the world around you. You feel that your life will only have meaning when you are helping other people. You will feel incredibly happy even if you have only touched one person. You will feel like your journey here has not been in vain. And many of the activities you used to love will no longer hold any special meaning to you. You have a new purpose in life and new goals. You need to contribute something to the good of the world around you.

Questioning the Status Quo

When you begin to have a greater connection to your true self, you will start to look for answers for your purpose in life and even your very existence. You might begin to question all of the ideas you once took for granted. You might change your focus from the pursuit of money or other forms of instant gratification to looking for experiences that have depth and meaning. Your perspectives will alter, and you will look for purpose in all things. This journey can lead you into painful dark places even while you begin to feel liberated from the person you used to be. The problem with this part of your journey is that you will not be able to truly heal until you can acknowledge the source of what has wounded you in the past. As you begin to awaken, you will make the connection between your current behaviors and your past experiences. You can't indeed become enlightened unless you are willing and able to confront the darkness in your life and consciously acknowledge it.

Diving into your inner psyche to confront your shadows and demons can be difficult to do, but you will need to if you want to continue to grow and develop. You need to know where you came from to be able to understand where you are at this moment in time. When you can do this, you will be able to step into the future and find the self you were meant to be. When you begin to awaken to your true nature, your ego will face certain death, and it will attempt to do everything in its power to keep things as they are, to maintain the status quo. Your ego is the false self that you created with your mind. It does not truly reflect the person you are, the person that is emerging during your transformation. Your ego will cause you to try to revert to your previous behaviors. When your spiritual practice leaves you suffering, you might feel more attached to your old self. But you need to question the status quo and let your ego die so that you can achieve real awakening.

While you are in the process of Kundalini awakening, you will form new perceptions that will be entirely different than your current view of the world. You will feel a lot of doubt, and at times you might doubt your sanity. You will reveal some new things about yourself that will be in direct contradiction to those things that you have always believed. As you get deeper into your Kundalini awakening, you will more closely align with your higher truth. You will begin to attract energies from the Universe that will help you create your new reality. These energies will help light the way for you when the journey becomes too dark for you to want to continue.

Your status quo believes the things you have always considered simply because you have no reason not to accept them. You find yourself complying with the old way of doing things. You follow your beliefs because you have always believed them. When you begin your Kundalini awakening, you will be forced to question the status quo. Questioning is the only way you will be able to grow spiritually. You will not achieve your full transformation until you question the reality of now so that you can move on to the new self that you will become.

Streamlining Your Life

Making your life less cluttered and more streamlined does not just apply to physical clutter, although that is an essential part of streamlining. When you have experienced your Kundalini awakening, you will no longer feel the need to surround yourself with things that have little or no meaning for you. You will need to take some time to look at the objects that fill up your home and question whether or not you need everything that you see. If you are holding onto something that you no longer use, something that gives you no pleasure, then get rid of it. Your house is probably full of things that you don't even recall why you have them, so get rid of them. After the transformation, you will naturally desire a simpler, less cluttered life, and this will begin with your physical possessions.

An even more massive drain on your energy is mental clutter. There are three main areas in which mental clutter will manifest itself in your life, and those are busyness, aspirations, and the overload of information. Part of your mental clutter might be tied up in your physical mess, in the form of books and magazines you mean to read one day, movies you have never watched, and that pile of recipes you have never tried making. One rule that cleaning experts use is the six-month rule: if you haven't used it in six months, then you don't need it. Get rid of it. Unfulfilled aspirations are another area of mental clutter that you will no longer have time or energy for after your kundalini awakening. Think of all of the good intentions you have that you have never gotten around to starting. Then look at them and decide if you still want to do all of these things. Your Kundalini awakening will take you to a place where you will demand simplicity and order, and there might be things on that list that no longer hold any meaning or interest for you. And you should try to reduce the control that social media has over your life, as much as you possibly can.

The worst kind of clutter is the emotional clutter that is present in your life. After your Kundalini awakening, you will find you no longer desire to spend your time on meaningless social obligations. You will no longer do things just because you feel obligated to do them. You will also no longer worry about being forgotten or neglected if you don't take part in every social obligation, as you did before. You will want to create new expectations for yourself and new patterns of behavior. You should never attend a social commitment just because of your feelings that you should. After your transformation, you will only want to do the things that are beneficial for you, and this will let you live a more streamlined and peaceful life.

When you have undergone your Kundalini awakening, and you are free of physical, emotional, and mental clutter. You will no longer waste precious time trying to manage things, people, and situations that should not be an issue in the first place. You will feel lighter and happier. You will suddenly find that you have more time for the things you want to do and the people that you want to see. And you will be loaded with an abundance of energy that will help you reach all of your goals and see your desires through to completion.

Connection with the Divine

There are many names for the Divine energy that is the Kundalini. The Great Goddess or the Divine Feminine is also known as Shakti, the spiritual guide that desires to lead you to reach your very own spiritual pinnacle, your own Nirvana. All people are the vessels of this force of life, no matter their background or culture or anything other designation that might define them; the Divine is in everyone. Even more than energy alone, Shakti is also the location of wisdom, mind, and strength. When you decide to awaken your Kundalini and take the path that will lead you to the force of Shakti, then you will be arousing your calling to the Divine.

What she is will be found within you, and you are what she is. She is just waiting to be awakened from her coiled state at the base of your spine, which she will be able to do when your Kundalini begins to rise through the central channel. She will travel through all of the pathways in your body to help you break through your blockages and clear out all the negativity in your body. Her ultimate goal is to drive you straight to oneness with the Divine. Connecting to your unique essence will serve to awaken your Kundalini as Shakti rises within you ultimately.

Once you have awakened your Kundalini and Shakti has risen to consciousness within you, it will be time for you to connect with your Divine Self. Doing this will provide you with harmony, peace, guidance, and an illuminating light that will come to you through the higher knowledge you will receive. It will now be much easier to turn away from the temptations of the physical world and turn your attention to the power, love, and light of your eternal Self. This will help to reveal the attachments, desires, and illusions that are keeping you held to a lower path because you are on a lower vibrational frequency. The transformation will allow you to find your higher way that will take you to your true enlightenment. You will also more easily recognize those things that are disharmonious, restricting, and limiting the flow of positive energy through your subtle body.

The Divine is always looking for ways to reach you so that He can send you wisdom, love, illumination, and the power to draw higher situations, feelings, and thoughts into your life. The Divine is a wise entity that is ready to show you a better and more joyful way to live. Because of all the good things that are waiting for you, it will not be hard for your subtle body to connect with the Divine. You will only need to set your intentions to connect with the Divine and your own Divine Self. Then you will be open to all of the gifts of consciousness that are awaiting you as you make contact.

Begin by setting your intention to connect with the Divine and to be genuinely open to the inspiration, love, and energy that is waiting for you. During this part of the process, you need to be still and silent. Connecting with the Divine goes far beyond the boundaries of your mind, so you will need to be somewhere that is as free of distractions as possible. Your full powers of receptivity are required to be able to connect with the Divine. So release any random thoughts you might be having. Imagine that you hold all-knowing wisdom, unconditional love, and infinite intelligence. Let your mind be still. Turn your concentration from the outside world to the power that is within you, because that is where you will find the Divine.

Try asking for something from the Divine, some sort of insight or guidance. The Divine will impart the most extensive parts of love, power, and wisdom when you are quiet and peaceful because this is when you are the most receptive. After spending some amount of time in silence, notice how your thoughts have changed. Notice the new feelings you have that are centered on abundance, wisdom, and spiritual visions. You might even receive a message internally that sounds as though it is coming from you, but it is the Divine working through. Do not get discouraged if you don't hear or feel any messages at first, because it may take time to make contact with the Divine fully. Connection with the Divine comes in many different forms. It might be in your deeper breath, an inner knowing, an answer to a question, or a fantastic rush of energy if you do not feel any kind of response that is perfectly fine because your intention to make contact with the Divine is also a form of connection. Some new inspiration or insight may have been given to you, and it will be revealed to you when your time is right for it.

Humans are intended to show the power of the Divine and connect with the Divine. Once you have awakened your Kundalini and complete your transformation, then you will be that much closer to reaching the Divine and your self-realization.

CHAPTER 5

Your Metamorphosis In Four Stages

You will encounter a period during the Kundalini awakening that is often described as being the darkest night of your soul. It is that time when you are at your lowest, just before the transformation to self-realization begins. During this time, you will most likely endure moments of deep despair, times when you feel intense fear, and you will probably wonder why you thought this would be a good idea. Most of these feelings will come from your personality because they are the result of you finally dealing with and identifying with your character.

Because you identify with your thoughts, your personality will be the main focus of your mind's eye. When you speak your opinions and believe that they are correct, you are identifying with your thinking. The story that you are telling will make you feel energetically alive. When you are awakening your Kundalini, your thoughts will turn dark, and this will create a dark vibration in your soul and your body. Once the dark vibration has taken hold, it will continue to send little waves of dark thoughts throughout your mind and body. At this point, you will be temporarily hooked to the dark vibrations, and your soul will be trapped in the circle of reactions between the dark that exists and the light you are seeking.

Your Kundalini will rise because you want it to. You have a spiritual yearning for something better than you have now. The part of yourself that wants to know yourself entirely is the part that will call the Kundalini to rise and take action within you. The method that you use to awaken your Kundalini is not the critical part, because the ultimate result will be the same no matter how the Kundalini is awakened. The energy will push through the blockages in your chakras as it seeks to fill and conquer the central channel and rise to the Crown Chakra.

It is relatively easy to compare the Kundalini awakening to that of a flowing river that has been flooded by heavy rains. As the river becomes saturated, the water will begin to flow through places where it has never gone before. It will creep out into new territory, rearranging the land on its quest to conquer a new area. The same thing will happen to your subtle body when you begin to awaken your Kundalini. The flow might be small at first and difficult for you to notice, but it will eventually grow and develop into a mighty flood that will encompass your entire body, mind, and soul. Because your spirit, body, and mind all intersect in your subtle body, you will be able to experience the results of your awakening on any or all of these levels.

The process as a whole will be different for everyone who undergoes a Kundalini awakening, but several major stages in the awakening process are familiar to everyone. It might take you weeks, or months, or maybe even years (at the longest) to experience some of these stages. The amount of time that passes will depend on how intense a particular Kundalini shift is inside of you. If you feel that you have many changes throughout your lifetime, it might be that you are experiencing one long growth with many smaller cycles throughout your life. The possibilities for how a Kundalini awakening will play out within you are infinite; the number is as endless as the vast number of people who desire to undergo a Kundalini awakening. The process is unique to the individual. The purpose of any guide into this transformation is to give you some guidelines to follow that can help you to progress on your path correctly. It will help you to process the changes and be able to integrate your Kundalini shifts into your progress.

The first stage you will experience in your awakening is often referred to as the burst and bliss stage. Bliss, a feeling of overwhelming happiness, is one of the most intense byproducts of Kundalini awakening. It will feel much like a light in liquid form as it flows through your body in powerful, but gentle, waves that crash and subside. This feeling might happen while you are meditating, or it might happen spontaneously sometime during your day, even though it is a wonderfully ecstatic experience, which should not be the main focus of the experience. While you should enjoy the blissful feeling when you have them, you should not try to stay with them or to recreate them when they are not happening naturally. Let them run their course so that you do not get stuck in one spot of your transformation. The feelings of bliss are the means to the end, not the end themselves.

Kundalini energy shifts might also manifest themselves initially through bursts of physical energy. You may have random periods where you feel very restless, and you feel the need to move continuously. You might find yourself swaying or shaking a body part, like swinging your leg or tapping your foot. Your body is merely trying to process the sudden rush of energy that is flowing through it. When your Kundalini begins to shift, it is much like increasing the level of watts to an electrical appliance. Your physical body is the outlet or the circuit board that is receiving the energy, and it will need to learn how to handle the sudden surge of energy. Your best course of action during this time is to find ways to take care of yourself. Eat nutritious foods, exercise when you can, and try to keep yourself well-grounded in reality. You must be able to grow and develop before you can rise to the next level.

In your next stage, you will experience growth spurts. When your Kundalini goes through its different shifts, you might feel just like you used to think like a child when you were growing, and nothing fit the right way. You will begin to feel like nothing in your life provides you any longer. This feeling might seep into one or more areas of your life. You might start to feel stagnated in your career. You might think that you have somehow disconnected from your friends. You may feel that your wardrobe is outdated, and your home furnishings look suddenly shabby. You might even begin to prefer different colors and different foods than you used to. Your life might feel constraining and old to you, where before your experience was entirely satisfactory to you.

Your internal set point has shifted. Your awareness of your life and your base of perception are different than they were before. You are beginning to form the person who will be the new you, and the old you is beginning to ebb away and disappear. At this point in your transformation, you will have two distinct choices for your path. You can embrace the changes you are experiencing and look forward to what lies ahead, or you can try to pick up the pieces of what is left of you and stuff it back into your old reality. The progress of the remainder of the stages in your transformation will be directly affected by the decision you make at this time.

You will find the path in the future very difficult to navigate if you try to go backward in your transformation. If you can embrace the changes that are happening to you, then you will be able to move forward. You will find the ability to develop reasonable goals for your transformation, and then you will be able to achieve those goals using compassion, clarity, and wisdom. When you reach the end of your shift, then you will realize the goal of a beautiful new life, and it will more closely resemble the new person that you are becoming now. Whatever you eventually decide to do, you will need to make your decision with conscious thought. Many of the people who are in this stage of transformation tend to make hasty or rash decisions. There will be very many times when you will need to make a quick decision to determine your next steps, but this is not one of those times. Right now, you need to take time to consider your options and take slow steps toward your eventual change.

After major shifts, you might tend to feel acutely frustrated, and this is also quite normal. Part of this pain and frustration comes from the fact that your spiritual rates of change and your physical rates of change happen quite differently. The material world moves so much more slowly than the spiritual world does, and you might have a mind full of unique ideas that you would like to manifest without the ability to do so. You will need to follow the proper sequences and take all the steps in order as they come.

When the Kundalini awakening begins, and you are going through shifts in your transformation, you might start to feel that you are on a wildly energetic emotional rollercoaster. You begin to be extremely sensitive to the feelings of other people, and you may suffer from extreme mood swings. Sometimes women will feel these changes more acutely than men will. In the male body, the Kundalini rests at the base of the internal chakras, near the Root Chakra. But in women, the Kundalini is sleeping near the second inner chakra, the Sacral Chakra, which is closely linked to the feminine emotional body. Their subtle body also tends to be more sensitive than the subtle body of the male. Women are usually more likely than men to experience strong mood swings and wildly fluctuating emotions.

You are experiencing the effects of two major shifts when you reach this point in your transformation. New energetic and intuitive abilities are most likely being unleashed as your Kundalini begins to move through your body. You may have the ability to suddenly see things that you were not able to see before. You will also be much more aware of the subtleties of energy in your environment and the people around you. As you begin to develop your new skills, they may become genuinely psychic abilities with skills for healing. They may also be overwhelming in the beginning, as you learn to adjust to the rush of new sensitivities. You will find these adjustments much easier to make if you take some extra time to pamper yourself and take care of your personal needs.

The growth you are experiencing might make you feel resistant, as though you don't want to change, and this can contribute to the emotional swings you are having. You can feel an overwhelming rush of old attachments, insecurities, and fear that rise up inside of you. You may think that you are sliding backward on your path as if you have dealt with these feelings before, and they should be gone now. These are often nothing more than the residual bits of the old patterns of emotional response that have been stuffed down into the deepest parts of your subtle body. The flood of the Kundalini coursing through you has brought them floating to the surface, stirring them up so that you can face these old emotions head-on and get rid of them for good. You can work through this stage by practicing meditation, spending time soul searching and self-inquiry, and writing your thoughts and feelings in a journal.

The heart of the shifting process during the Kundalini awakening is often compared to a school for life teachings. Your mind and spirit are looking for the lessons that they feel you need to learn. Your life will settle down into a new pattern after every shift. During this time, you will experience new ideas, or old ideas in a new disguise, that appear in your life demanding to be addressed. You might face some new opposition in your quest to reach a specific goal. You might need to develop some new goals if you decide that the old ones just aren't working for you any longer. You might face new challenges in your relationships, or you might feel the need to seek out new relationships. You may find yourself in life situations that seem foreign to you because your thoughts and feelings have changed, and parts of your subtle body that have not surfaced before are now on display.

The last shift might have stirred up a lot of old emotional baggage, leaving you with an abundance of emotional residue. There will be even more emotions and thoughts kicked up by the challenges you will face during this stage. While this may feel traumatic in the beginning, it will become less and less painful as you go through more shifts in your transformation. As you progress further into your Kundalini awakening, you will find yourself resisting the changes less and less. Your lessons will become happier and gentler as you begin to look forward to your new abilities. You will learn that growing mentally and emotionally does not need to be painful. Usually, it is your resistance to the growth process that makes it hurt so much.

Now you need to remind yourself that you are experiencing exactly what you asked for. You wanted to undergo a Kundalini awakening. You knew the benefits that would come to you by awakening your Kundalini and going through the transformation. You are going through this entire process in the first place because you had an overwhelming longing for a higher spiritual connection and a desire to grow in all matters. Spend some time enjoying this journey you have undertaken. Try not to dwell too much on the pain you might be feeling, but think about the result. You will be able to help yourself through these changes by reminding yourself of the new wisdom and compassion you are feeling. Think of the supercharged connection to the Divine you will soon be enjoying. A new level of liberation and happiness is right in front of you, and you are being given an excellent opportunity to grow and develop.

The final stage of your metamorphosis is the integration process, but you usually will not notice this part as its separate stage. It is not marked by any significant changes, so it is often overlooked. If you take the time to look back at the person you were before, then you will be surprised to see the changes that you have gone through to get here. You have a new energy level and a new perspective on life, and you are more comfortable in your new transition. You are enjoying a new level of understanding and peace in your life now that you have let go of the old emotional residue that was holding you back in your previous life. On some basic fundamental level, you have reached a new level of maturity.

In one way, your Kundalini awakening will never ultimately end. As many times as you try to seek a new level of spiritual maturity, then you will never entirely complete your shifts. You can find yourself deep in the throes of a new cycle as you are completing the one you are currently in. You will have time to regroup and rest when you are in a lull in the activity, enjoying a period of quiet. You can always choose to slow your growth for a while if you need some time to recuperate. Your spiritual desire will let you know when it is ready for another round of awakening and growing.

Some things will remain constant as you are going through your cycles of change and growth. There are distinct phases to every layer of your transformation. When you first become attached to a new layer, then that is your starting point. But since you are continually transforming, you will eventually become dissatisfied with that phase, and you will be miserable. This is your cue to begin the move to the next phase by letting go of this phase. Once you can drop the attachment to the phase you are in, you will begin another spiritual awakening in which a higher self will emerge. The transformation is fueled by the tremendous amount of energy that is released. Spiritual reactions and profound healing will accompany the biological aspect of the transformations. You might have feelings of one or more of the charismatic symptoms that are associated with spiritual transformation. You might experience weight loss, amplified hearing, telepathy, repressed memories, visions, insights, sudden clarity, out of body experiences, tingling in your body, numbness, flashing lights, and strange noises. These symptoms are mostly due to the changes you are experiencing in your nervous system, as well as your body and your mind. In the days following a spiritual awakening, you might feel enormously elated. You will feel awake and more spiritual because of the direct contact with your higher self. You will never be completely able to forget the wisdom and insights that you received during your revelations, and you should not try to forget them. You will be permanently changed by your Kundalini awakening, and that is the ultimate goal. You will look at the world differently because your system of values has changed.

When you go through the different phases, you may find yourself dropping attachments you had to certain things, places, or even people. Your internal healing will continue even when the joy of your new position begins to settle down. You might experience intense emotions, or you may feel pain in various parts of your body. You might have days when you feel completely exhausted. You might have dark thoughts for several days in a row. Your consciousness might become flooded by the memories of your past life, and you may have disturbing dreams. You might not feel very well physically, and you might be regretting your decision, feeling that you have made many large sacrifices and gained very little to nothing for your effort. During your awakening, every part of you is undergoing immense changes, so you will need to be patient with yourself. This is not the time to undertake anything strenuous.

At the end of your Kundalini awakening, you will choose to surrender to your higher self, the new you that is part of your self-realization. In this context, the act of surrender means to divert your energies from your old habits of acknowledging your personality and into your new way of life that is free of any ego. You can use meditation to quiet your inner voice that comes from the mind if it has not entirely transformed. Your new higher self is that part of you that will work to heal you when it is needed. Your spirit must make the first changes in your new self because your body is merely a reflection of your spirit. If you allow your mind to remain in control, then your transformation will never be complete. When you surrender to the Kundalini awakening experience when you accept the changes that have happened, then your higher self will win in the end, and your transformation will be complete.

CHAPTER 6

Life After Kundalini Awakening

Once you make it through the fires of change and emerge on the other side of your Kundalini awakening, then you will have some period of adjustment. You will need to be able to integrate your new life into whatever part of your old life that you are keeping. You will not be ready to rebuild your life immediately after your transformation. You are feeling different realizations and feelings, and you probably are not sure of who you are now.

You will feel an extraordinary intensity of change inside after your awakening. It is impossible to understand if you have not experienced it yourself, so other people might not know what you are experiencing. When you go through a Kundalini awakening, it is something like experiencing an internal fire, and in the first period after the awakening, you need to let the fires burn down. The burning will eventually subside, and you will be able to begin your rebuilding process. You may not have dealt with all of the issues that were dug up during your awakening, and that is okay. You can always revisit these at a later date, as long as you do not allow them to become a part of you once again.

As human beings, you are an amazing and fascinating creature. When you learn to get out of your way, then you will be an amazing person. You will naturally flow towards the things that support you and are meaningful for you. There are many ways in which you will need to grow up all over again after your Kundalini awakening. All people who experience the transformation will walk a different path because the journey is completely personal. You have cleared out space inside of yourself, and you might be content to simply sit back and observe where you are going and what you are doing and saying. You will begin to get an idea of the kind of life that you want to live while you are enjoying this natural state of affairs. Your soul will intuitively want to live the best possible life. Once you have begun the adjustment process, then you can start to take the actions you need to take to begin to move toward your new life.

This process will be completely different than your old methods, where you consciously plotted every move that you would make. You might do some of that while you are figuring things out. The space in your soul after you have cleaned it out in your awakening will embrace anything you introduce to it. Your soul is a curious entity. No ability or possibility will be left out in your search. Everything in the world is now available to you. This will give you the ability to decide how you want to create your new life and what you want to have in it. This method will only work when you are spiritually awakened, so if you have tried this before with poor results, then don't be afraid to try it again. You are not actively seeking to arrange your new life; you are not actively planning anything right now. You are simply living while your higher self decides what direction your new life will go in. Your intellectual, emotional, and physical tendencies are to try to move back into your old way of life with your old patterns of behavior. Those situations will only reveal what your subconscious mind relates to and not what your new natural, curious soul wants to explore.

In your new life, you will try, and you will fail, and this is perfectly normal. You are learning how your divine intelligence is supposed to work. You can't control the process or even predict how it will go because you will need to take action sometimes and allow life to flow on its own sometimes. You will alternate between receiving from life and taking your actions. You will make mistakes, especially in the beginning. You will know times when you will sit back and receive things when you should be acting, and other times when you should wait to receive what you are trying to act. At those times, the new life you are trying to build will feel like it is falling apart. Be patient; everything will work itself out.

Life after a Kundalini awakening might feel a lot like a mid-life crisis. All the things you have previously committed yourself to have been taken away or are being dissolved right before your eyes. Everything in your life is open for review. Your career, your dietary habits, your family connections, your relationships, all of your old addictions and habits, everything you knew before and understood might now be gone, or it won't mean the same to you. If you react with fear and resistance, then your integration process will be stagnated. Your journey is just beginning, and you will need to meet it with discipline and courage.

You might experience various physical symptoms after the awakening. You might feel overwhelmingly energetic. You might have obvious physical symptoms like periods of trembling, an inability to relax, and visual disturbances. Your symptoms might be more emotional, like feelings of despair, depression, or anxiety. The amount of energy that is coursing through your body after the awakening strains your nervous system to the extent of its limits. Some people will experience a steady and slow onset of symptoms, and some people will experience them in a great rush. Do not let yourself obsess over what you are feeling now, but try to find different methods for relaxation and let the process take its course. The channels of energy are now open, and your body will eventually heal itself. Look for ways to treat and heal your entire body, and try not to focus too much on the individual symptoms.

There may be an overwhelming desire to try new things. You might finally be willing to seek out new situations. You might finally be feeling the courage to do so, or the desperation to leave your old life behind and move on to the new one. These feelings can be quite intense. Some people try new diets, change their jobs, or look for new careers, or even leave established relationships. All of these changes are nothing more than an attempt to deal with the new energy inside of you. And while you are willing to try new experiences, you will be available to receive new kinds of support from unexpected sources. You will eventually meet the right kind of people, you will find the right kinds of classes to take, and you will learn the new skills that you need for your new life. When new things are meant to happen in your life, they will.

When you begin to make the changes you want to make in your new life, you might find that you are more sensitive to some things that you used to tolerate simply. You will need to be more cautious about the things you bring into your life. You might need to spend less time on social media. You might need to begin a new exercise program or experiment with some dietary changes. Listen to your body, because it will let you know what it needs to be whole and healthy. As your nervous system continues to adjust and change, in its drive to accept the new levels of energy that are coursing through it, you will be even more sensitive than you were before. This is a clear sign of future potential and increased awareness, and it is not a sign of weakness.

You will also find that you are more aware of what is happening around you, and you will be more sensitive to the environment that you are in. You will develop a deeper relationship with your soul, and you will pay much more attention to your intuition. You begin to rely more on your inner compass so that the opinions of others no longer mean to you what they used to mean to you. You will become aware that your body needs some special attention and that your chakras might need unique tuning. You will naturally react when you don't feel grounded or comfortable within your skin. You will know what you need better than anyone else will, so you will become your own best healer. This might include a daily practice of meditation or yoga or some other form of exercise. You need to spend some quality time every day with your deeper self, taking time to look beyond your ego and your personality. You will need to use whatever tools you have to allow yourself to evolve and heal.

When you originally become more aware of your new self, you will also be more aware of the part that you play in the workings of the larger world around you. You will develop a heightened sense of compassion for other people as you learn to love yourself more. Your heart is now opened to the sufferings of other people. This will give you the desire to help other people, especially those who are going through their own awakening process. You have an inner knowing of the connection you have with the rest of the world. You will also begin to feel a deeper connection to nature, now that you feel more comfortable in your own body. You will want to care for others while you are caring for yourself.

And you will have an immensely growing sense of purpose in life that will begin to influence you in ways you never thought possible. This is your real destiny. You will be ready to deliver your destiny when you have made the connection to your soul and your heart, when you can channel your energy in positive ways, and when you can get beyond the traumas of your past to be able to heal yourself. You will now know your connection to the Divine, and you can freely express yourself. You will fulfill your destiny by elevating yourself when you can give freely of yourself from your heart. You will work to make the world a better place, and you have a renewed spirit of energy and purpose. You will have realized the true purpose of a Kundalini awakening, and that is the ability to live honestly in your mind and spirit.

CHAPTER 7

Methods For Awakening The Kundalini

If you can sit quietly, closing your eyes, and breathing deeply, you will probably be able to feel your pulse. If you are still, you might be able to feel the energy buzzing around in your body. That is your Kundalini, looking for an outlet. This deeply revered and universally acknowledged energy that pervades your everyday life is waiting for you to unlock it and let it flow. Your Kundalini is an energy that rests at the bottom of your spine like a small coiled serpent. When you release this energy, it will flow freely upward through your chakras to give you an expanding state of your consciousness and a deeper connection with the Divine. This is what is known as a Kundalini awakening.

When you awaken your Kundalini, you will be more balanced spiritually and emotionally as well as being more inspired and creative. The energy of the Kundalini supports your spirit and drives all of the everyday functions of your mind and your body. This awakening has been practiced in India for thousands of years and was brought to the western world as a form of yoga practice. The practice of yoga was originally taught to people as a way to find true spiritual enlightenment. Modern yoga is more concerned with poses, but true Kundalini yoga will help you in your quest for true spiritual enlightenment. Kundalini yoga wants to incorporate the focus on all parts of the person into one holistic practice. This means that energy release is taught for the spirit, mind, and body all at the same time. The physical poses will focus on the key points of energy in the body that will activate the areas that need assistance to allow the energy to flow freely. Specific techniques for breathing will help you to unlock your inner energy and learn to control your breathing. The physical part of the Kundalini yoga practice will help you to achieve a heightened sense of awareness.

Kundalini meditation will help you awake your higher consciousness and the energy of the Kundalini. While you are meditating, it is important to breathe properly to attain peace. Practice breathing directly into your tailbone, since this is where the Kundalini is coiled and waiting for its awakening. While you are breathing, try to direct the breath you are taking down through your spine and then back up, all the way to the top of your head. Focus continually on the upward movement of your breath. Then let the breath cycle down to your heart, and then back up. Complete your cycles of breathing with some sort of mantra or chant while you are focusing on the breath.

Kundalini Yoga

Since your body is a complex system that holds vast systems of energy, it will need specific methods of yoga for energizing it. Kundalini yoga was developed centuries ago for the specific purpose of awakening the Kundalini by opening the seven internal chakras.

Unlock the Root Chakra with the Crow Pose. Stand straight and tall with your feet close together and your arms stretched out in front of you, palms facing down. Slowly drop to a deep squat, with your bottom almost resting on the floor. Hold it for five seconds and then slowly come back to a standing position. Keep holding your arms straight out in front of you the entire time.

Unlock your Sacral Chakra with the Frog Pose. Leave your toes planted tightly on the ground and lift your heels, keeping them close together. Set your hands on the ground in front of you and look forward. Inhale deeply through your nose and then straighten your knees while you drop your head toward the ground. Then let out your exhale as you drop back into the squat.

Unlock your Solar Plexus Chakra with the Stretch Pose. Lie on your back on the ground or a yoga mat. Lift your feet about six or seven inches off of the ground and lift your head off the ground. Bring your arms up beside your body so that they are in the air just above the level of your hips. Breathe deeply and slowly.

Unlock your Heart Chakra with the Camel Pose. This pose needs to be done carefully so that you do not strain your lower back. Kneel down on the floor, with your leg from your knee to your feet on the floor. The top part of your feet will be resting flat on the floor. Bend backward slowly and grab your ankles with your hands, allowing your head to drop back and down as far as possible. If you are not able to stretch that far back, then place the palms of your hands on your hips near the small of your back and stretch back only as far as you feel comfortable doing.

Unlock your Throat Chakra with the Cobra Pose. Lie on your stomach on the ground. Put your hands flat on the floor right under your shoulders, with your palms lying flat on the floor. Push straight up with your arms, lifting your heart and letting your head follow, but keep your pelvic area on the floor. If stretching this far is too much for you, just come up part of the way.

Unlock your Third Eye Chakra with the Guru Pranam Pose. Kneel down on the floor with the top part of your feet on the floor, and sit back on your heels with your spine straight. Bring your torso down over your thighs and let your forehead rest on the ground. Lay your arms on the ground in front of you, so that they are extended flat in front of you.

Unlock your Crown Chakra with the Sat Kriya Pose. Sit back on your heels and stretch your arms straight up over your head, with your fingers pointing straight up. Let your elbows hug your ears. While you hold this position, chant the words 'sat nam' over and over; slowly and carefully. Keep your eyes closed. This particular yoga pose will work to open up all of your chakras. It will specifically work to wake up the energy of your Kundalini and help it to work upward along your spine and through your chakras.

Keep in mind that there is no best pose, and no one chakra will stand on its own without the others. The entire chakra system works together in an interrelated and holistic system. You can't work on just one of the chakras and ignore the needs of the others. Your Lower Triangle of chakras, the lower three, deal with things that need to be eliminated from your body. The Upper Triangle of the upper three chakras focuses on the accumulation of energy in the body. The two triangles meet in the middle of the body at the Heart Chakra, which works to balance the forces between the chakras.

Kundalini Meditation

While the exact origins of Kundalini meditation are not known, the traditions date back to about three thousand years ago. The word Kundalini translates to a coiled snake. This refers to the belief that everyone has divine energy that they carry coiled up at the base of their spine. The practice of Kundalini meditation works to awaken the coiled snake, release it, and harness the energy for the good of the human. Besides awakening, the Kundalini, practicing this form of meditation will also promote greater mindfulness, relieve stress, and help you to become more mindful and aware of your body and its place in the world.

The most important purpose of the meditation is to move the energy of the Kundalini through your body. The concept states that the energy that is coiled at the base of your spine will need to be released to travel through your seven internal chakras. Releasing this energy will create a communication system between your body and your mind. This communication will work to relieve your spiritual, mental, and physical issues. Bringing awareness to all parts of your body by getting you connected with your breath is meant to help you to be more present in your current time and space, help you establish a smooth new rhythm, and assist you in communicating with the higher version of yourself.

Kundalini meditation is not a system of beliefs. It is a practice that you will do daily to cleanse your spiritual body and your mind. It will help you counteract physical tiredness and manage the stress of daily life. It will also work to calm your mind and balance your chakras so that you are no longer simply reacting to the stimulus in your environment, but you are acting with purpose in your life.

Follow the steps of Kundalini meditation carefully. Start with a basic form of meditation and work to a deeper and longer meditation once you have mastered that form. This is not a race or a goal but a practice. Since it is better, to begin with a small routine, pick a time length that is manageable in your current schedule. You can always adjust later. You will feel overwhelmed if you try to do too much too quickly, and this could sabotage your efforts. You can do just five or ten minutes each day, and you will receive benefits from it.

Choose the location for your meditation. While you can do your meditation anywhere, you will want to be in a spot that is quiet and free from distractions. This should be somewhere that is peaceful and relaxing for you. If you can set aside a regular spot, then you might want to put some of your most favorite things there. Dress in clothes that feel comfortable for you. Since everyone has their idea of what is comfortable, there are no special outfits that you will need to have. Many people who practice meditation prefer to do it in some flowing, loose garment that is soft to the touch. You will need to feel comfortable so that you will be able to get into your practice easily. You might want to drape a soft cloth over your head to enhance the feeling you are trying to create.

Many people like to practice early in the morning to get a good start to their day. Others say practicing at night, just before going to bed, helps them to relax and sleep deeply. This is also left up to your personal preference. Since your body will be busy digesting your food, it is not recommended that you meditate directly after eating. Where you sit during meditation is also your choice. You can sit on the floor with your legs crossed, as it is often a picture, or you can sit in a comfortable chair. Not everyone is able to sit down on the floor and get back up with ease! The main point in where and how you choose to sit is that you need to sit somewhere that your spine will be straight and upright.

Your practice can last anywhere from five minutes to three hours. Again, this is also determined by you and your needs and your schedule. Maybe you can do a short meditation before beginning your day, and then a longer one just before bed to help you relax. There is no one correct answer. You will need to choose your mantra. This is the saying that you will repeat, out loud or in your mind, to help you focus during your meditation. The mantra should be something that you will feel comfortable saying. Its purpose is to direct your focus and your energy during meditation. Once you become comfortable with your mantra, you may want to think it to yourself at various times when you feel stressed, as a way to help you calm down. The main point of your mantra, besides helping you focus, is to help you break out of your old patterns. It needs to reflect the state that you want to be in, not the state that you are in.

Focus on your breath and let it slow down gradually. Your goal is for each round of breathing, and inhale and an exhale, to least about eight or nine seconds. Always breathe through your nose. While you are practicing your breathing, focus on how the air is moving through your body, and helping you to relax. If your thoughts begin to wander, just bring them back to the present by focusing more on your mantra and your breathing. Have a timer already set so that you are not watching the clock while you meditate, if you are on a time schedule. Complete your session of meditation by taking a deeper breath as you slowly raise your arms above your head, to release any final toxins that might be lingering in your body. Then exhale and relax.

Increase the length of the time that you meditate gradually as your schedule allows. Watch for the energy moving along your spine as you focus on your breathing. Even if you can only manage two minutes of meditation at first, then you are doing just fine. You will need some amount of practice to be able to clear your mind and focus on your breathing, especially if you are highly stressed in your daily life. Eventually, you will find it easy to enter the state of meditation, and then this will work its way over into other areas of your life. You will find that you are not so reactive during the day, and that little annoyances don't annoy or aggravate you the way they used to.

Chanting

Chanting can be an easy yet powerful way to awaken the Kundalini inside of you. Chanting is often referred to as a practice of yoga for your mind. When you are chanting a mantra, you are trying to reach one of three levels of consciousness. If you speak the chant out loud, then you are trying to activate the physical level of your being. When you whisper the mantra in your chanting, you are looking for love, someone to belong to, and inner peace. When mantras are thought and not spoken, they are guided toward the divine in you and the other worlds. Do things that you can do to make your mantra more powerful for you. One of these is to visualize the mantra being written while you are saying or thinking it. The other method is to listen to the word actively while you are saying it.

The purpose of chanting, especially when it is done as a part of meditation, is to close out the outside world and have a few minutes of peace with you. Choose your mantra carefully because you should know the meaning of the word, and it should mean something to you. Try one of these mantras that are used for chanting

- Ohm is probably the one mantra that comes to people's minds when they think of chanting. This word means that it is, it will be, or it will become. Its specific sound makes

it the sound of the universe. The word itself represents the cycle of life and death and reincarnation.
- Satchitananda, or Sat Chit Ananda, is a compound word in the Sanskrit language. Sat means being present or being alive. Chit means to acknowledge, feel, or comprehend. Ananda means happiness, joy, or bliss. So when it is said all together, it means that the chanter is present in the feeling of joy, or another comparable phrase.
- Aham-Prema will help you bring together your soul, mind, and body in a feeling of great peace. It helps clear distractions from your mind and leaves your past in the past. It means I am Divine love.

You can also write your mantra for chanting, as many people like to do. This will make it specific to you and what you need in your life. Think of a few things that you are craving mentally or spiritually right now. It might be love, peace, forgiveness, or one of many other things. The mantra needs to be said in a positive tone. You would not say 'I am not afraid,' but you would say 'I am strong and brave.' While this might feel strange to you at first, relax and give it time to develop. Chanting a mantra, just like yoga or meditation, are practice and not a goal.

Teacher of Kundalini

Some people who will assert that you should never try to awaken your Kundalini on your own because it is too dangerous, that you should always have the assistance of a trained teacher to guide you along your path. If you feel that you will need to have someone like this in your life, it is your personal preference, but it is not really needed.

There is nothing dangerous about awakening your Kundalini. The danger that many people see is the opening up of old wounds and old traumas that might cause a strong negative reaction within you. You will not be able to rise to full enlightenment until you are able to let go of the past. Simply acknowledging a past trauma will not be enough. You will need to examine it for what it was, acknowledge the effect it has had on your life, and then be strong enough to let it go. Many people hold onto old wounds as some sort of security blanket. As long as this problem is with them, then they will not need to function above a specific level in life. Kundalini gives you the possibility of living a pure, high-functioning life, but to do that, you must purge your soul of all of the old darkness so that you can step out and walk in the light of the Divine.

So if you feel you need a teacher for your Kundalini awakening, look for one who has been helping people successfully and is willing to work on your schedule and at your pace. Some people move easily into enlightenment, and other people take longer. You will need to deal with the darkness as it comes, and you will need to do this at your own pace. But when you have achieved full Kundalini awakening, when you have cast off your old life and stepped into the light of the new day, you will feel completely fulfilled.

CONCLUSION

Thank you for making it through to the end of *Kundalini and the Chakras*; let's hope it was informative and that it was able to provide you with all of the tools you need to achieve your goals whatever they may be.

The next step is to take the information that you learned by reading this book and apply it to your own life. If there is any part of your personal life that is not measuring up to the way you expected it to be, then that might be a sign that you need a Kundalini awakening. Just the mere fact that you were curious enough about it to read this book means that you are seeking something more in your life, and Kundalini awakening is just the thing that you need.

Use the information that you have read to begin working on yourself and your own transformation. Remember that the way will now always be smooth, and you will need to be prepared to deal with things you feel are better left alone, but in the end your mind and your spirit will be filled with a kind of peace that you have never known in your life. A Kundalini awakening will provide you with this peace and the energy to maintain your glorious new life.

Finally, if you found this book useful in any way, a review on Amazon is always appreciated!

Kundalini

Ultimate Guide to Awaken Your Third Eye Chakra, Develop Awareness and Spiritual Power Through Kundalini and Chakra Awakening

Laura Connelly

INTRODUCTION

Congratulations on purchasing *Kundalini*, and thank you for doing so.

The following chapters will discuss your Third Eye chakra and the immense meaning and ability it will bring to your life when it is fully opened and functioning correctly. Your mind and soul will flood with light and love from the Universe. The world around you will become brighter and more intense than ever before. You will find yourself filled with the knowledge of all things and all of the power that the Universe will bring to you in your daily life.

Your sixth sense is present in your Third Eye chakra, and it holds your ability to see all the mysteries of the world and to live in harmony with the Universe. You will know things you have missed before and feel feelings you never knew were possible. Having fully opened this chakra is vital to your ability to use your intuition to see through the drama and illusion that may cloud your world at times. It will allow you to navigate your life on your terms, no longer being dependent on half-truths and imagery when you seek reality.

And having the Third Eye chakra fully functional will allow you to travel to other planes and communicate with the beings who reside there. The wealth of the entire Universe will be yours to sample and enjoy as your conscious mind receives messages from the Divine and other sources of spirituality.

There are plenty of books on this subject on the market, thanks again for choosing this one! Every effort has been made to ensure it is full of as much useful information as possible, please enjoy!

CHAPTER 1

The Third Eye Chakra

Inside your body, placed along or near your spine from your tailbone to the top of your head, are your seven internal chakras. Your Third Eye Chakra is in the center of your forehead, between your physical eyes. Your body will communicate on a subtle level with all of the energies around you. Certain of these energies will directly relate to a specific part of your body. Of the seven internal chakras, the sixth in line is the Third Eye chakra. It directly correlates to your psychological abilities, mental skills, and how you evaluate your attitudes and beliefs. This chakra is connected directly to your pineal gland, pituitary gland, and your brain. This chakra is linked to your mind. It is responsible for your unconscious and conscious psychological tendencies as it resonates with the energy of your psyche. It is the chakra that houses your sixth sense, wisdom, and intuition.

Location and Function of the Third Eye Chakra

Everyone has a Third Eye chakra, and everyone can open and access their Third Eye chakra if they choose to do so. You might be using it without even knowing that you are. Whenever you get that little feeling that something isn't quite right with a person or a situation, when your gut tells you something you find difficult to ignore, then that is your sixth sense in action. Your Third Eye is giving you the perceptions it has collected so that you may act upon this knowledge. Even if you are not immediately able to locate the source of this information, it is still valid and should not be ignored.

The Third Eye chakra is challenged by the need to discriminate between the source of your thoughts and feelings, and whether these are motivated by illusion, fear, or strength. You will need to develop a mind that is impersonal and find the ability to detach yourself from mental and physical illusions. To be able to know what is in your soul, you will need to transcend your thoughts, fears, and worries. Your Third Eye chakra will drive all of these functions. It holds a combination of memories, personal experiences, fears, and facts that are all unique to you and your experiences. All of these are continually active in the energy of your subtle body, which is also known as your soul.

The foundation of all the wisdom you will ever possess lives in your Third Eye chakra. It deciphers the difference between what is true and what you believe to be true in any situation. Negative memories can manifest within your mind and become truths in your later life. If an adult told your child self that you were stupid, your adult self would most likely believe that you are a foolish person. This example is just one example of a feeling that is valid to you, even though you can't produce the facts to support your theory. Your Third Eye is another sense organ that can be improved with work, and one of the things that it will do is help you dig through your opinions to find the facts behind them. It will also help you receive the vibrations that other people put off, and this will help to enhance your perceptions of life as you learn to choose who to be with and who to put aside. The person who made you feel stupid by calling you stupid might be one of those you would set aside, or at least you will know how to deal with them in the future.

Your Third Eye chakra finds its basis in truth. Many of the ideas that you currently think of as truths are nothing more than the remnants of prior negative experience, like being told you are stupid. Once you have opened your Third Eye and can see the real truth, then you will be able to rid yourself of these incorrect preconceived notions. This chakra wants to break down the stereotypical ideas you are holding on to. The world feeds you illusions, and you will be able to detach yourself from them. Your freedom will allow you to think freely and control your thoughts. There will be no limitations that you will not be able to conquer when this chakra is opened.

You will learn that there is no one person or group of people in society that will have the power to determine the path that you will walk. A larger karmic entity will now drive your life and your decisions. Until you can use the full energy of your Third Eye chakra, you might believe that the findings and opinions of other people are the keys that drive your actions, but this is just a psychic illusion meant to hold you as a captive in situations that are not healthy for you. Currently, you create karmic manifestations that cause you to suffer from illnesses or feel pain in your life. The opening of your Third Eye will help you move beyond all of that.

Psychic Abilities

Not everyone knows how to use their psychic abilities, especially in adulthood, although everyone is born with the knowledge. Children see and feel everything because they have not yet learned that there needs to be limitations on what they can see, hear, and touch. Once children turn into adults, they usually lose the ability to tap into their psychic powers because their minds have become closed and jaded. Life's experiences have taught adults to mistrust their own better judgment, to the point that they are barely able to function on their own in the real world.

People who use their psychic abilities daily are no different from you; they have just learned how to have an intuition that goes beyond the boundaries that outline the physical world; they can taste, sense, feel, hear, and see things that most people are unable to perceive. Most people have what is deemed to be the normal perception by the guidelines of society. For most people in most situations, the perception of reality is a factual matter. You can tell when someone is not feeling well physically, and you will agree with most people that the sky is blue with white fluffy clouds. When you begin to expand your sensory abilities, you will find out that most people do not use many of the senses that are available to be used. You will become more aware of your inherently unique psychic gifts when you come to this awareness.

Psychic skills are the ability to process the sensory data that comes from both intangible and tangible sources. You will find yourself able to process this data on an intense spiritual, physical, or emotional level. This is a broad definition because psychic gifts tend to vary significantly in their application and intensity. You will enjoy a sense of oneness with the Universe when you open your Third Eye chakra and use it regularly. The main focus of many of the spiritual practices is achieving this oneness because then you will have unlocked the powers of your Third Eye and your psychic abilities.

Telepathic Awareness

When your Third Eye chakra is open, you will be able to receive thoughts or feelings from another person over distances, and this is known as telepathy. Using telepathy does not involve using the basic five senses of sound, sight, touch, smell, or taste. With ESP, you know something without having direct contact with it. Everyone is born with the ability to be telepathic, just like everyone is born with the power of psychic abilities, but it takes conscious effort to keep these skills in use. Many people are not able to learn to use their telepathic powers because they view telepathy with mistrust and skepticism, and this keeps them from being fully able to develop their talents.

You must be well relaxed when you are trying to use your telepathic abilities to communicate with others. Your mind will need to be open and receptive to receiving information. If you continue practicing your skills at receiving messages from others and sending messages out to other people, you will eventually be able to do it with minimal effort. Envision the recipient standing with you and having a regular conversation, and use words and phrases that show great detail. Keep trying to send out your message until you feel that it has been received. As you practice more, you will become familiar with this feeling, and you will know when your intended recipient has gotten the message you are sending. When you first begin receiving notifications, they may appear as sudden thoughts, and you might be tempted to ignore them. Listen to these messages, even if you don't act on them, because this is the beginning of the lines of telepathic communication opening for you. News will come to you in various ways. You might receive feelings, thoughts, images, emotions, and desires, and these are all normal and indicate that the other person is sending messages that are full of great detail. Sometimes people can receive notices when they are asleep.

When you begin using your powers of telepathy to send and receive messages to other people, you will start to communicate with other people on a deeper and more meaningful level. You will find you have a greater understanding of others. And this form of communication will work anywhere and anytime, in any situation, so it makes sense for you to develop this ability. When you become more assertive in your practice, you will even learn how to block those people from whom you don't want to receive any messages.

The human brain is hardwired to be able to pick up subtle cues and messages from other people, although most people never use these abilities. Your mind can also send out your emotions and intentions to other people. Some people are more capable of using the power of the Third Eye chakra simply because they want to; they practice regularly and honestly believe in what they are doing. Your Third Eye chakra is the seat of all of your wisdom and knowledge and your link to the Universe. The light of the Universe is the element of the Third Eye, and its theme is the desire to see and to know all that is possible to know.

CHAPTER 2

The Third Eye And Psychic Abilities

Inside your physical body is your subtle body, the spiritual part of you that receives messages from the Universe and sends messages back out. Your Third Eye chakra is what is responsible for your imagination, clairvoyance, concentration, intuition, and psychic abilities. To receive the energies of the Universe, you will need to open your Third Eye and be fully connected to it. This chakra is at the very center of your sixth sense and the source of all of your psychic powers.

Your sixth sense is the intuition that allows you to read the future as well as the past and the present. It will enable you to receive non-verbal messages from the other side of the veil, that cosmic covering that separates the living world from the world of the non-living. You will receive messages from loved ones who have gone on before you, angels, and spirit guides. You will also use your Third Eye when there is an intention that you want to manifest in your life. A purpose is an idea or a desire, and displaying merely means to make it a reality in your life. Your intention might be to lose twenty pounds, and the manifestation is when you take steps to lose that twenty pounds. You will use your Third Eye to visualize your intention, to see it as being part of reality.

Except for the Heart Chakra, which is the center chakra and the balance between the lower three and the upper three chakras, the chakras all have balancing chakras in your subtle body. The balancing chakra for the Third Eye is the Solar Plexus chakra, the center of your gut feelings. When these two chakras are opened and balanced, they will work together to enable you to cruise freely and smoothly through your life. You will still encounter difficult times and other obstacles along the way, but these are just the steps in your personal and spiritual growth. Even when you experience difficulties, you will be able to learn from them quickly and grow and move on, without finding yourself stuck in that particular situation for very long. When this chakra is open, it will give you the power to have a strong intuition, spiritual focus, and mental clarity.

ESP (Extra Sensory Perception)

This ability allows you to receive information with your mind. This will include the capabilities of telepathy, intuition, psychometry, clairvoyance, precognition, and retrocognition. There is also the ability that is known as the second sight, where you might learn things that are not readily available to your five senses; you might receive knowledge through a vision or a dream state. ESP is your sixth sense, the power of your Third Eye. You will feel information in your gut as well as in your soul and your heart when you are receiving information using ESP. This form of psychic power, like the others, has no boundaries of time or space. You might be able to manipulate physical objects, see into the future, and know the thoughts of other people. You may experience ESP in many different ways.

Precognition – This is the ability to see into the future direction so that you will know people, places, and events before they ever happen.

Retrocognition – This is the complete opposite of precognition, because it allows you to see into the past, and especially into the distant past. You will be able to recognize past events and people that you were not part of in real-time.

Déjà vu – This involves feeling like the recent experience that you are having is an experience that you have taken part in before. With this type of ESP, you will know the details of events you should not be able to understand.

Telepathy – This is the power that allows you to know the thoughts of other people. This ability can be used to communicate with others without ever writing or speaking.

Telekinesis – This is the power to physically affect an object by using the capabilities of your mind, without ever touching the object.

Mediumship – This is the one ability that most people refuse to use because it involves communicating with deceased entities. Mediums channel the energy of the departed and receive messages from them, and then they relay those messages to the people who are waiting here in the world of the living.

Relaxation and Emptying the Mind

The idea of emptiness is another way to look at an experience that you are having, a different way to perceive matters to help you understand them. Emptiness will not subtract from or add to the actual raw data of the experience. It will allow you to use your mind and your senses to make conclusions without wondering if there is any backstory or confidential information. This type of thinking is called emptiness because it has none of the suggestions that people usually add to an experience to try and make sense of the experience. It enables you to see the world as it is and to make sense of the events of the world that you live. People will often create mythical stories to try to explain an event or experience that they do not understand, but emptiness will eliminate that habit. When you create a view of the world to describe an adventure, you interfere with the knowledge and your ability to understand it and resolve it, because your attention is drawn away from the critical information that you need.

When you adopt the practice of relaxing and emptying your mind, then you will be able to view an experience or an event without reacting to it. You will watch the event as it happens, and you will feel no emotions in what you are seeing. You will merely try to determine what the event means in your life if it has any meaning at all. Not all of life's experiences and events will have a sense in your life, and emptying your mind will allow you to determine which experiences warrant further attention from you. You will see the truth in the event without feeling emotions.

It will take you time and practice to master the art of emptying your mind and learning to relax. The first instinct of most humans, when they face a new experience or event, is to react to the situation immediately. You will need to learn how to remove yourself from reaction and concentrate on viewing what is happening. Spend some time every day; focus on the ideas and perceptions that you hold as truths. See which of your thoughts you can get rid of, because this will help you empty your mind, and a clear mind is a relaxed mind. Lose your preconceived notions and assumptions about your views and stories. Removing these from your mind will remove suffering and stress since it will be eliminating anger, greed, and delusions. Your mind will be clear, free from the garbage that is limiting your psychic abilities.

Parallel Worlds

When you have activated your Third Eye chakra and your psychic powers are healthy, you will be able to interact with entities in parallel worlds. These worlds do exist, and those entities already interact with people on Earth. There is important evidence that points to the existence of parallel worlds. In the world of quantum physics, it is suggested that every possible outcome of a particular situation will happen. Still, they will all happen on different planes and in other Universes. Only one conclusion can occur in each Universe. To allow this theory to be a reality, there would need to be as many parallel worlds as there are possible outcomes to a situation. There is also the idea of the multiverse in physics. If we believe that our Universe began with the Big Bang, then it is possible to think that many other Universes started with a similar Big Bang. While some people say there is no concrete evidence that other worlds exist, there is also no substantial evidence that proves they do not exist.

In the center of your physical brain, there is a small gland, about the shape and size of a small pine cone that is known as the pineal gland. Ancient teachers believed that the pineal gland was surrounded by a substance that was much like vapor and was the point of entry into the soul of the human. We know now that the pineal gland is part of your endocrine system, and its job is to secrete the hormone melatonin, the hormone that is responsible for controlling your circadian rhythms, those regular cycles of sleeping and being awake that is ruled by the presence or absence of light and dark. The pineal gland does not produce melatonin when there is discernible light, so people sleep at night and stay awake in the daytime. The melatonin that the pineal gland secretes is the hormone that induces sleep.

Mystics and seers once revered the pineal gland because they believed that it had some control over the Third Eye chakra. Since they saw that light and dark guided the human in their sleeping and waking, and since they knew that all entry into the human soul came through the vapor surrounding the pineal gland, they believed that the pineal gland was somehow involved with bringing information from outside the mind to the soul inside of the body. The pineal gland is a sensor that specializes in detecting the changes outside your body and makes the necessary internal changes to make physiological adjustments. The pineal gland gives you the feeling of well-being when it works harmoniously with your Third Eye so that you feel a heightened tendency toward spirituality. Your Third Eye attaches you to your subtle body, as it is the bridge between the spirit world and you. Your Third Eye will see the reality that is beyond what your human eyes see, especially in matters relating to entities in parallel worlds. The doorway to all psychic and spiritual values will be open to you, and you will be able to use lucid dreaming, telepathy, clairvoyance, and astral projection as you wish.

Astral Mind Travel

Depending on the tradition that it is referring to, astral mind travel can go by many different names. Whether it is known by one of the western terms of dream body, celestial body, or energy body; or the diamond body of Taoism, the Egyptian ka, the Buddhist light body, the subtle body of Tantric tradition, the Hindu body of bliss, or the Christian experience of the different heavens, it is all a form of astral mind travel. The human body includes the physical structure and the subtle body, and it is your subtle body that is active while you are dreaming and is responsible for projecting astrally. Your out-of-body experiences are the combination of your dreams and astral projection. When your subtle body is well cultivated, then it will be able to survive the physical body as a model for consciousness.

Astral mind travel is also known as an out-of-body experience or OOBE. These can be intentional, or they can happen involuntarily while you are sleeping. You can also trigger an OOBE by depriving yourself of water and food, or if you are sick or you suffer from some physical or mental trauma. Lucid dreams make excellent opportunities for astral mind travel. You begin the experience by observing your sleeping form after you have left your body. Practice will allow you to be able to direct your awareness to particular locations or activities. Your subtle body is the area of your form that will do the traveling. Your rational mind and your physical body are linked to one another by your subtle body, the intermediate body of light that travels the astral planes. When your celestial body is having an OOBE, it is crossing the astral planes of other Universes.

Astral travel also validates the existence of life after the death of the physical body. When you have experience with astral travel, you will be completely aware of yourself outside of your physical body. You will be able to touch, hear, smell, see, and taste from the area around you.

When you are deeply in meditation, soundly sleeping, or engaging in conscious astral travel, a switch is activated that allows you to travel on other planes. This switch is the activation of the pineal gland, which releases chemicals that cause your subtle body to leave your physical body, whether you are consciously traveling astrally, deep into your meditation, having a lucid dream, or at the point of death. And having your Third Eye chakra open and healthy is necessary for all of this to happen.

Since your subconscious is in control of your soul while you are sleeping, you have no amount of control over what happens unless you have a lucid dream. If you are doing so, then you can have a heavenly mind experience and travel out of your body. There are some benefits for you to practice astral mind travel consciously. You will be able to travel well beyond the boundaries of the physical world and its rational thought processes. Your inner spiritual being will blossom, and you will experience a definite boost in your astral abilities. You can enjoy a complete transformation of your perspective of yourself as a spiritual and physical being in this world. You might find that you will operate with a greater sense of consciousness in the daily activities of your life after you experience astral mind travel. The reason for this is that you are now secure in the knowledge that you are more than just a mere physical being who is doomed to live a boring life and be forgotten after death.

It is reasonably simple to prepare your body to have a heavenly mind travel experience. This is often best done in the early hours of the morning because it is easier for you to reach the relaxed state of being and heightened awareness that is needed. This can also be done just before you fall asleep for the night. Astral mind travel is a personal experience, so have your experience when the time is right for you. Do this when you get into bed since your physical body will need to be completely relaxed. And since astral mind travel is a personal experience, it is best to prepare for it when you are alone. Keep the room dark and silent and get rid of anything that might distract you.

Lie flat on your back and clear your mind. The goal is for you to reach a state where your mind and body are completely relaxed. Breathe in and out, slowly and evenly. Try not to think of anything, either thought about your day or thoughts about the travel you are about to take. If you have a crystal to clear your Third Eye chakra, you can place it on your forehead while you are relaxing. Let your physical body, and your subtle body get close to the edge of sleep, but do not allow yourself to fall asleep just yet. For astral mind travel to occur, you will need to be at that thin line between being awake and being asleep. Keep your eyes completely closed, and your focus on one part of your body. Try to make that part move by using only the power of your mind. Keep broadening your focus until you have included your entire body in your direction. Continue until you can proceed forward with your whole body by using the power of your mind.

Now it is vitally important, more than ever before, for you to remain relaxed because you will likely feel a series of movements like little waves as your soul gets ready to leave your body. If you feel any fear at this moment, your soul will not go and you will not be able to engage in astral mind travel. Let the vibrations of the waves carry you while you continue to remain relaxed and peaceful. Use the power of your mind once again to move your body to a standing position. As you stand up, take a look around the room that your physical body is lying in, then walk across the room and turn and look at yourself, all while using just the powers of your mind. If your physical body can feel you looking at yourself from across the room, then your experiment was successful, and you are ready for astral mind travel.

You might want some concrete proof that you are engaged in astral mind travel. Go into another room and move an object, looking at it closely before you set it back down. Then when you awaken, you can physically go into the other room and find that object. When you have completely mastered this technique, then you have mastered astral mind travel. Eventually, you will want to travel to new locations that are not as familiar to you. When you travel, always try to mentally record details of the places where you go, so that you can go back and look for these places later. When you use astral mind travel to go to unfamiliar places, they will seem familiar when your physical body goes there. Astral mind travel is perfectly safe, and you will always return to where you came from.

Controlling your Dreams

You might have already experienced a lucid dream. If you have ever been dreaming, and then suddenly you told yourself that this is a dream because you were sure that you were dreaming, then that is a lucid dream. If you have ever controlled the storyline that the dream had, then that is also a lucid dream. Most people dream all of the time and never know that they are dreaming until they wake up and recall parts of the dream. Lucid dreams happen during periods of rapid eye movement, just like all other dreams do.

Lucid dreams usually happen spontaneously, although it is possible to train yourself to have a lucid dream. The ability of people to control their dreams varies widely. Lucid dreaming is a process that will let you explore the worlds that are inside your mind even while you are entirely aware that you are dreaming. There are many practical applications for the use of lucid dreaming in real-world situations. One way to use lucid dreaming is for people who have recurring nightmares to grab control of the nightmare and change its course consciously. You are less likely to be afraid of something that you can control. You can also use lucid dreaming as a form of entertainment because it will allow you to travel anywhere and do anything that you want.

There are things that you can do if you want to practice lucid dreaming. One method of testing your dreaming is called reality testing. This will help you to verify whether or not you are in a dream. While you are dreaming, check the time on a clock, and recheck it several minutes later. If you have a lucid dream, the time will fluctuate wildly, not go at a natural pace as it does when you are awake. For your dream to be considered a lucid dream, it will need to have four common characteristics. You will need to know that you are dreaming, the things you see in your dream might disappear when you wake up, your dream will not follow any standard rules of physical laws, and you know that there is another world that is outside of the dream world that you are in. The dream does not need to make sense; you just need to be able to understand what is going on in the dream. For example, if you dream that you can flap your arms and fly through the air and it makes sense to you in the dream, then you have a lucid dream. It doesn't matter that people really can't fly, since the physical laws of the real world do not apply in the lucid dream.

Lucid dreams work in four stages, each one being more profound than the step before. The first level is the normal level of non-lucid dreaming, where most people begin. When you are in this state, you will have no idea that you are dreaming and anything that you see, you will recall later and accept it as being part of reality. You will not have any conscious control of your dream, and it will be entirely created from your mind. In the second level, you will begin dreaming of something that seems impossible in the middle of dreaming about something possible. Your unconscious mind is being blocked by something in your conscious mind, so while you might want to leave the dream, you are not able to. At this point, you are partially aware that you are dreaming and somewhat not. When you reach the third level of lucid dreaming, you will be able to have an utterly lucid dream as long as you are willing to accept the lucid dream. You need to realize that you are in a dream and be ready to stay there and experience the dream. The most important part of the lucid dream is not in control of the dream, but in being willing to play along with the dream. On the fourth level, you will be able to experience the end of the dream, whether it comes to a conclusion or ends, and you will wake up.

Developing your Third Eye is your doorway to all possible psychic experiences you could have. When this ability is cultivated, then the separation between spirit and self will dissolve. You will feel cynicism, jealousy, uncertainty, pessimism, and confusion if this chakra is blocked. The highest source of divine energy will come through an open Third Eye. Opening this chakra will bring you the ability to engage in astral projection and lucid dreaming. This will also give you an enhanced imagination and a better quality of sleep.

CHAPTER 3
Exploring The Spirit World

The spirit world is that realm that is inhabited by spirits, those spiritual manifestations that inhabit other parallel worlds. This external environment for souls is independent of the natural world that you settle, but the natural world and the spirit world are continually interacting with one another. These two worlds continuously communicate with each other through various methods.

There are many realms of existence beyond the physical world in which you live. The domains operate on different vibrational frequencies than this one because each part is on a different level of energy. When you travel between the realms, you will become aware of a change, a shift in the power from one kingdom to another. The spirit realms also do not operate like the physical realm in which you live, where many different people make a melting pot of humans and their characteristics. In the spirit world, each domain is the location of spirits who have achieved a particular level in their spirituality. When people leave this physical realm, they do not immediately become saints or angels. People who pass on will retain their personality and memory, and they will continue in much the same form as they did when they were alive, but in one of the spirit realms.

When you leave this physical world, you will go to the realm that you deserve to go to, a plan which is based on how you lived your life in this realm. This level of spirituality will be reflected in the vibration of your aura. Your vibrations will be higher if you have been a spiritual person in this realm. You will then pass into the realm that most closely matches your vibrational level. These inhabitants of these spirit realms will visit your physical realm, and they encourage communication between the domains.

Clairvoyance

This word translates into a clear vision. Clairvoyance is the ability to learn information about a person, object, location, or event by using your psychic abilities and extra-sensory perceptions (ESP). People who use ESP are clairvoyants who use the power of clear sight to see persons or events that are in distant time or space. There are three different abilities that all fall under the umbrella of prophecy. Remote viewing is the perception of events that are currently happening that are outside of your normal range of perception, like events that happen far away. Precognition gives you the ability to know or predict future events, and retrocognition is the ability to view events that are from the past.

Clairvoyants will see things with their mind's eyes, using their sixth sense through their Third Eye chakra. The real talent of the clairvoyant is the ability to determine the meaning of a message or an image that they receive. This enables them to decipher the vibrations that other people emit as well as receive notifications from the spirit world. Many people are clairvoyant without realizing that they are, but they will display certain traits or talents. If you have mental images randomly flash into your mind, if you see visions in your mind that look like a movie is playing or if you get flashing images of numbers, colors, symbols, or other images, then you may have clairvoyant abilities. This is especially true if you see flashes of colors or bright lights, as these may be angels or spirit guides trying to communicate with you to send you a message. Since prophecy has a lot to do with seeing mental or physical images, visualization is a big part of being clairvoyant.

You might be able to assemble an object without reading the direction or repair a small appliance because you can see in your mind how the item should operate. You might never get lost because you have a marvelously innate sense of direction. You excel at assembling puzzles, completing mazes, and reading maps because the tasks that require visual traits and spatial abilities are your specialty. You prefer jobs that allow you to use your sense of creativity, and you dearly love beautiful things. Your dreams are often really vivid due to your overactive imagination. If you have some of these traits, or even if you don't but would like to develop them, then you can do some or all of the following exercises.

Meditation – The practice of meditation is essential to being a clairvoyant and to opening your Third Eye chakra. When you practice your meditation regularly, you will develop your psychic gifts and improve the vision of your Third Eye. You will be able to clear your senses, raise your vibration, and get out of your logical mind.

Keep a Dream Journal – Clairvoyants will usually have vivid dreams, and writing them down in a notebook is an excellent way to develop your abilities. When your logical mind is at rest, your subconscious mind takes over, so that it is free to receive messages from the spirit world. Sleep time can be a great time to play when your subconscious mind is making connections with the spirit world and engaging in astral travel. It is a good idea for you to keep your dream journal right beside your bed. This will allow you to write down your dreams the moment you wake up while they are still fresh in your mind. You can also plan to receive messages from the spirits by merely setting an intention while you are falling asleep.

Playing with Crystals – Crystals are invaluable to anyone who is working with their chakras, their aura, or developing their psychic abilities. Use a crystal to open your Third eye, and to keep it open and healthy. Put a crystal on a table near you while you are meditating, or hold it in your hand gently. Put the crystal on the table next to your bed when you sleep. While clear quartz will work on any chakra, a piece of amethyst or fluorite is both renowned for their ability to heal your Third Eye chakra. Other good choices for crystal therapy for the Third Eye chakra are aquamarine, opal, emerald, and celestite.

Play Games that Encourage Clairvoyance – Simple games will help you strengthen your clairvoyant abilities while you are having fun playing them. Play the card game 'memory.' To play this game, you will lay all of a deck of cards face down, and then you will turn them over two at a time, looking for pairs of the same card. Have a family member or friend set a group of ten unrelated items on a table. Study the things for one minute, and then leave the room. While you are gone, the other person will remove one of the items and hide it out of your view. When you return to the room, you will need to tell which item is missing.

Practice Visualization – the Clairvoyants, will need to have strong abilities for visualization, so this is one trait that you will need to practice. Clairvoyants see with their mind's eye, their Third Eye, so all of the visions, pictures, and symbols that you see will be in your mind. You will find it much easier to receive images if your Third Eye is open and functioning correctly. Take some time every day to visualize different photos, scenes, and pictures in your mind. Relax while you are doing this and try to have fun with it, using images to create images in your mind.

Premonitions

Spirituality is based on the awareness that you are connected to something greater than yourself or your ego. This something greater goes by many different names, depending on the beliefs of the particular person. Religious people might refer to the higher power as the Almighty, God, Yahweh, Buddha, or Allah. Those who are not believers in one formal religion but consider themselves spiritual creatures might refer to the Great Spirit, the Absolute, or the power in the Universe. And some people don't refer to any name at all but prefer to think of the higher power as a sense of infinite beauty and fantastic order. Whether you label it or not, that something greater provides you with a sense of meaning and strength in your life.

As people mature spiritually, they will often find that their power of knowing and seeing expands. These elevated abilities often include the capacity to understand events that have not yet happened, events that are in the future. There is a long line of seers, shamans, visionaries, and prophets that will attest to this possibility. The modern version of this ability is now known as the sixth sense, gut feelings, intuition, or hunches.

Premonitions have a deep connection to spirituality, especially when the suspicion involves someone we love or care deeply about. Premonitions will open you up to other people and the rest of the Universe. They show that you are part of something much larger than yourself, that you are an element in the fabric that connects all the beings in your Universe. Premonitions reveal the oneness that exists when minds are linked across time and space. They are proof that you are not an isolated individual, but a person whose individual consciousness operates outside beyond your physical body. They suggest that you are infinite in time and space. Premonitions are the window through which you can see your connection to the Divine.

You can test your hunches to determine whether or not your suspicions are real. Before you know who is calling on the phone, try to guess who the caller is. Try to imagine what a store will look like on the inside while you are still outside of the door. The ability to know these things is not luck; it is premonition. When you experience déjà vu, do not be afraid of it because there is nothing scary about it. Déjà vu is merely telling you that you have knowledge of this place or person before you are physically there, and that is a premonition. People often ignore that nagging feeling in their gut, but you should not, because that is just a suspicion that something about this person or situation is not right.

Many people will experience their premonitions while they are dreaming. They can see the people who are involved in the situation and the situation itself. This is known as having a premonitory dream. Your mind is showing you something that will happen in the future in real life. If you can have this kind of vision, then you can be susceptible to events that are not easily explained in simple terms. You are probably more intuitive and open-minded than most people you know. The most significant difference between regular dreams and premonitory dreams is that premonitory dreams are based on real situations. You will find yourself in a situation watching people do things, and it could be part of a dream, and it could be happening in real life. In a vision, the events of the dream are created from your mind, and you are in control of the events of the dream. When you have a premonitory dream, the events of the dream will come to you, and you will merely watch them unfold, as though you were watching a movie on a screen. You will have no control over the dream. And these are easy to recall when you wake up because premonitory dreams are informative and very vivid.

There is a definite reason for your sixth sense being activated, as it is in a premonitory dream. The dream is trying to give you information so that you will be aware of a coming situation and you will know what to do when you encounter it. When you sleep, your mind is free from the restraints of the physical world, and it is open to go in whichever direction it chooses to go. If a particular premonitory dream keeps returning to you, it is best if you pay attention, because your spirit guide is trying to tell you something.

Daydreams

The act of daydreaming is allowing a steady stream of conscious thoughts to keep you from doing those things you are supposed to be doing, or it might merely be a way to pass the time pleasantly. It will direct your attention inward to personal and internal matters and away from the external issues that are surrounding you. Almost everyone daydreams, and no two imaginations are ever identical in content. Fantasies serve to assist you with thinking about the future, thinking creatively, and thinking of new ways to deal with old issues, refreshing your attention span, and thinking creatively.

Daydreaming is an excellent release from boredom. Daydreaming will allow you to let your thoughts wander during those times when you are engaged in some tedious task, or you are somewhere you would rather not be. Sometimes the stimulus coming in from outside is repetitive and causes you to tune it out with daydreaming. This lets you relieve the strain on your mind by mentally stepping away from the repetitive information so that you can return to it when you want to. If you are facing several different problems at the same time, you might want to daydream about different outcomes for the situations. This will allow you to switch your thoughts between other streams of information if you have several goals you need to plan for. Creativity is increased in people who daydream, especially in those people who daydream while they are trying to solve a complicated problem. When you use daydreaming about speculating about future events, you will have the opportunity to plan your reaction to them and their possible conclusions. This will also help you keep your mind off your goals while you try to plot the course of action that is the best for you to reach them.

Man has long been interested in the workings and wanderings of the human mind. Your brain comes with a built-in default network since it is made up of specific structures, and all human brains are built the same. The system in your mind will link several areas together to create sensory experiences. These experiences cause the brain to think about things that are apart from the events that are entering the mind from sources outside of the brain. Daydreams and fantasies are other words for the unique workings and wanderings of your mind.

Daydreams are not just useful tools to keep you from being bored, but they have practical purposes of serving. They allow you to explore your inner thoughts and ideas. Daydreams are particularly useful when you are trying to contemplate your past experiences, creating images of events you hope will happen to you in the future, trying to decipher the thoughts or actions of other people, or if you are faced with an ethical or moral decision. The default network in your brain makes your daydreams possible, and the nature of the dreams will have a direct effect on your soul and your mind. People often daydream about something they want but do not have, such as a partner or a better job. You can use your daydreaming time to help yourself in various ways.

Turn off the default network in your brain when you need to focus on something, and allow your mind to daydream. You will learn new skills or concepts better and faster if you daydream a bit while you are learning. Use your daydreams to write a unique life story for yourself, especially if something about your actual life is unsatisfying to you. Daydream about your current situation and create ways to make it better. You will perform better in your daily activities if you daydream about things that are familiar to you and not try to create new worlds for your mind to explore. And don't spend so much time daydreaming that it causes you to neglect your daily duties, but do allow yourself to daydream daily.

You will reveal much about your personality based on the details of your daydream. You are self-reflecting when you replay or rehearse your actions or thoughts during your fantasies. If your dreams are filled with negative thoughts about your life, then you might become mired in self-pity. Use your daydreaming to rewrite your experiences and make yourself the winner of every situation, as this will help you in your real-world life with others.

Your Personal Spirit Guide

There is an entity whose job is to help you, protect you, and guide you through your life. This is your spirit guide, and when your Third Eye is fully opened, then you will be able to find your spirit guide and communicate with them. This guide might be an ancestor who has gone on before you, an angel, or only a being of another astral plane which has been given the job of watching over you. They might have been with you in another life and need to continue until their job is completed satisfactorily. While you will have some sort of close relationship with your guide, communication is entirely up to you. The spirit guide is not allowed to make the first contact, but they can reach out to you after you initiate contact with them. They will guide you silently until then unless you are in great danger when they must step in to help you.

You need to fully believe in your spirit guide if you want to contact them. Most people will have more than one spirit guide. You are born with the one who will remain with you until you die, but sometimes other spirit guides are assigned to you for particular reasons. If there exists the need, you can always ask for more spirit guides to come to you. All of your spirit guides will work together for the common good of you. There are helper angels whose job is to wander the Universe in search of people who need them the most at any particular time. The Ascended Masters were once humans who passed on into the next realm and became leaders in the world of spirits. They will work to keep you safe and to guide your development in all things spiritual. You will have one Guardian Angel, and that is the angel that was assigned to you when you were born, who will remain with you until you die. The archangels are the assistants of the Ascended Masters, and they are also leaders in the spirit world. Archangels usually have one area of expertise they try to assist with. And sometimes one of your spirit guides will be your spirit animal, the spiritual embodiment of one of your beloved pets who has crossed the rainbow bridge. Your spirit guides will not contact you directly, but they will send you messages, like a dream to help you solve a nagging problem or a song that has special meaning to you. You can use different methods to communicate with your spirit guide once your Third Eye is entirely open:

- Improve your intuition
- Develop a spiritual practice of your own
- Use methods of divination like runes or tarot cards
- Daydream about your spirit guide
- Give a problem to them to help you solve
- Give them their unusual name
- Write to them in a journal
- Never stop looking for signs that they are with you

Mediums and Channeling

Of all of the forms of communicating with the spirit world, this is the one that is most often misunderstood and most often avoided. The medium connects with the spirit to speak, and the medium will be able to exert some level of control over the soul and how they act and what they say. Mediums do communicate with the deceased, and this is the part that bothers many people, but the spirits that are helping you are the spirits of dead people. How the medium and the soul will interact will depend significantly on the abilities of the medium, the intent of the communication, and the conditions the communication is taking place under.

When a spirit is allowed to control the medium, the medium enters a state of trance. The soul will then communicate through the medium instead of the medium, relaying the words and thoughts of the spirit to the person or people who called for contact with the soul. The medium at work is nothing more than a human instrument to allow the spirit to speak, a channel that the words of the soul can come through. The medium can help the spirit bring a particular message to the listeners. The soul is on the astral plane, and the medium is on an earthly plane, and the two beings communicate with one another.

Your physical eyes will show you what you need to see in the world around you, but your Third Eye will open up all of the possibilities of the Universe. A wide-open Third Eye will open your mind to the possibilities of life beyond the physical world. It gives you a unique sense that allows you to send and receive information at will. Your Third Eye will allow you to understand your connections with the Universe and those who live in it. And as these possibilities open up before you, will feel more powerful and more spiritual every day.

CHAPTER 4

Seeing Other Worlds Through The Third Eye

The astral plane, the world of the spirits, is inhabited by the spiritual manifestations of various entities, and it is known as the otherworldly environment for souls. This world is independent of the natural world that humans inhabit, although these two worlds regularly interact with each other. The entities of both worlds can communicate with each other across the astral planes. Humans have been looking for answers for centuries about the spiritual world. Man has learned many different ways to connect with and communicate with the planets that are beyond their own to gain higher power and spiritual knowledge.

The Art of Divination

The ability to foretell foresees, predict, or receive inspiration from the spirit world or a divine power is divination. When you practice divination, you are attempting to gain insight into a question or a situation by asking for information through a particular practice or ritual. You can make direct contact with a spirit or a god, or you can read signs, events, or omens. The method behind divination is to systematically organize all of the disjointed or random facts of the situation so that you can use them to provide you with insight into a situation or problem.

Divination has been used by oracles and seers for centuries to divine the truth from the spirit world. A prophet is a person who provides precognition or prediction using information that they received from the gods, to provide prophetic or insightful counsel to local leaders. The words of the oracle were deemed to be the words of the gods handed down for the leaders to act upon. Seers never spoke directly with gods as the prophets did, but their job was to interpret the signs the gods left for the humans. The seers used all of the methods at their disposal to obtain information, but they could not give detailed answers to the leaders as the oracles could. Through the sight of their Third Eye, they were able to provide solutions to the destiny of man. Using knowledge of past events and theories of future events, someone practicing divination can give insights into current events. When you have fully opened and engaged your Third Eye, there will be numerous methods of divination available for you to use.

Scrying has been used since ancient times, and it is one of the oldest methods of divination that is available to use. The traditional picture of a person practicing scrying is the old crone bending over her crystal ball. The word comes from words that mean 'to reveal' or 'to make out.' So the practice of scrying is all about revealing the things that are unseen by using your second sight and the power of your Third Eye. Your second sight will give you the ability to see something that can't generally be perceived by using your five senses.

Scrying will allow you to get in touch with your unconscious mind and all of the realms of your soul. It is a powerful form of analyzing yourself and understanding your intentions. Scrying is a beautiful method for getting in touch with your most personal goals, dreams, and needs if you are struggling with your purpose, meaning, or direction in life. Scrying is usually done by using some reflective surface, but there are other methods you can use for scrying. You can drip candle wax onto the water and then interpret the words or images the wax drippings form as they harden. Relax your vision and stare into a mirror, and then wait for the images to appear to you. Stare into a body of water and then read the images that you see there. Watch the flames of a roaring fire or the smoke rising from the fire for shapes and images. Gaze up at the fluffy clouds floating in the sky and see what ideas and forms are revealed to you.

When you are scrying, it is essential to be able to let your mind wander but keep your focus on the object, so it does require some amount of practice to become proficient at scrying. You need to allow your conscious mind to open and allow thoughts and feelings to flow freely through your Third Eye.

Dreaming of Symbols

Dreams are the messages that the higher powers of the Universe send to you, and they will often hold symbols and images that will bring you a particular meaning that is relevant in the natural world. There is an infinite amount of symbols and images that can come to you in your dreams. Anything that you can dream about can bring you a more profound psychological and emotional experience and significance than the item or event itself. If you dream about a house, it can carry many different meanings. A place might symbolize somewhere that you used to live, it might be something you want to achieve in your life, or it might carry a more profound meaning tied to an event in your prior life experience, especially in your childhood. Then you might have dreams where you are exploring different houses if you want to change something in your waking life. If you are craving the simpler life you enjoyed as a child, then you might dream about your childhood home. The key to understanding what the house is trying to tell you is tied to your reaction to the house. If you are seeking change and you dream about exploring homes, then the way you react to the homes will tell you when you need to keep looking and when you have found what you are looking for. Images and symbols in dreams do not have just one meaning, but some things are so familiar to see in dreams that they have acquired meanings that are generally accepted as the message they are bringing.

- A chase scene means that you are avoiding something important in your life; you are running away from something or someone that you need to confront and resolve.
- Water is indicative of the emotional state you are currently experiencing, whether the water is calm and peaceful or wild and crashing.
- Any kind of vehicle reflects an obstacle that you need to face or the direction you want your life to go to.
- Different people and different kinds of people in your dreams are reflections of your personality traits.
- When you dream of being back in school, you are looking for lessons in the events from your childhood.
- Dreaming about being paralyzed is an indication that you feel overwhelmed by something or someone in your life, or that you feel you are tied to a specific person or situation.
- Dreaming about death is not an omen of things to come, but an indication that something in your life needs to end or go away.
- Flying in dreams is the correlation of how you feel your life is going. The way that you are flying is a direct indication of the current path of your life, so flying out of control means that you feel your life is out of control.
- Falling is scary anytime, but in your dream, it is telling you that you need to let go of something that you are hanging on to in your life.

- You might fear feeling vulnerable if you dream that you are naked in a public place.
- Dreaming about having a baby does not always mean that you want a baby; it usually means that you are looking for something new and fresh in your life.
- Food can mean so many different things in your life. It might mean you need nourishment on an emotional or spiritual level. It might mean you are seeking knowledge or energy, or new insights into the way your life is going.

Etheric Entities

The ability to work with the entities of the etheric world is needed for your spiritual work. An entity of the etheric world is a being that is non-material and energetic. When you begin your process of awakening, you will have a great desire for new information. This new awareness will lead you through the darkness that is on the earthly plane and out the other side to the light of the other side. You will encounter the entities of the etheric as you seek for the new information that you desire. These entities will significantly differ in their form and power. Their level of energy is directly linked to their status in the spirit world.

You will have the opportunity to interact with many different types of etheric entities. You will encounter complex spirits, cultivated spirits, simple spirits, angels, disembodied humans, and deities. The many facets of the cosmos will be directly reflected in the different entities of the etheric. The larger fields of consciousness and power within the etheric realm are the deities. The various other spirits are more localized entities, and they are a smaller presence in the etheric realm. They can change their form whenever they want to. By interacting with the entities of the etheric, you will be able to draw upon a larger collective of energy and consciousness.

By opening your Third Eye, Chakra, you will begin to develop the skills that you will need to see these entities and communicate with them when you desire. To become aware of their presence, you will use your etheric perception, and when you want to share with them, you will use your etheric communication. You will be able to determine the kind of interaction that you will have with the entities of the etheric by assessing the nature of your personal goal, the type of entity that you are interacting with, and the particular relationship that you have with that entity. Your subtle body will determine the level of the relationship that you will have with the entities of the etheric. Your relationship will also depend on the particular entity that you are engaging in.

Cultivated entities are those simple creatures that were created by unique techniques to cast energy. They are also known as servitors, forms of thought, or artificial elements. When cultivated entities are sufficiently developed, they will be capable of showing the essential functions of the entities of the etheric. For reasons of practicality, they will often attach themselves to a material form. They prefer particular material forms such as paintings, clay figures, wax figures, statues, talismans, and crystals. They will infuse the material item with the essence of their spirit so that they can carry out simple tasks using elements of magic. These cultivated entities were created for the sole purpose of serving other entities, so they like to make themselves useful at all times. They are an external example of your consciousness and the force of your life as an extension of you.

Simple spirits have a limited amount of power because they are primal elementals and spirits of nature. They have almost no effect on the reality of the realm of the etheric, and they are most often encountered at the lowest levels of energy. Complex spirits have the power to affect validity. In ancient folklore, these spirits were known as elves, fairies, sprites, and demons. The complex spirits are natural allies for those who practice magic. The disembodied humans are nothing more than the souls of people who are deceased and are either unable to move on, or they refuse to move on.

The deities of the etheric world are the powerful ancient entities that human beings have been interacting with and communicating with for centuries. They are known as gods and goddesses in mythology and folklore. They exist as vast fields of complex consciousness within the etheric realm. Deities will often manifest themselves into human form because that is the form that is most easily seen by the human eye, and they need to be able to communicate with humans. You will enjoy a broader sense of consciousness and power when you can make a connection with a deity. While you are gathering strength from them, they will also be taking energy from you, along with your thoughts and emotions, because this is what gives them their power.

Inhabitants of the Astral Planes

When celestial bodies cross over from life on earth, they go to the astral plane. This is the place that is inhabited by angels, spirits, and immature beings. The astral plane is located two full planes above the physical plane that is known as earth or the material plane of being. A heavenly spirit is a being that has been separated from their human form, although they are free to take a human form and rejoin the people of earth at any time they wish. The astral spirits usually like to take on manifestations of their kind of design. You have probably encountered a heavenly being during your time on earth and not even realized you had an encounter.

The wonderful person you encountered may have been a succubus. When you are viewing the inhabitants of the astral plane, your human eyes are not useful, since they are often taken in by what they see. A succubus is a beautiful creation that harbors a dark interior. This creature will wait for your invitation to them since they prefer to take the passive route and let you be the aggressor. Then they will present themselves as the physical manifestation of your idea of the perfect beauty. When you enter a relationship with a succubus, it will be excellent at first, but eventually, the relationship will turn dark as the succubus begins to reveal their true self, but you will not have the power to see this until you are so far involved that you feel trapped. Ask the entity directly if you want to know for sure if you are dealing with a succubus. Celestial beings have no capacity for falsehoods, and they are not able to lie to you.

You probably encountered a fairy when you were a child because children can easily see into the astral plane. All of the innocents of the world are true believers, so they enjoy an active connection to everything they encounter in this world. The etheric creatures that reside in the world of the fairies are not just happy little creatures that fly around on ethereal wings showing their beautiful colors. All of nature is the residence of the fairies, and every aspect that is found in nature is represented by a fairy. The ancient being understood the fairies and believed in them completely. Fairies will happily coexist with all of the spirits in the astral plane and all of the humans on earth.

Your spiritual progress and growth will be inhibited by an archon. The spiritual energy that radiates off of the life forms of the astral plane and the earthly plane is the food for these parasitic creatures. Archons are so evil because they are angels who have fallen from grace.

They attempt to pass themselves off as sources of light and joy even though they are completely evil in nature. Archons want to infect everything and everyone with their evil intentions. They will do anything in their power to disrupt your spiritual progress.

Thought forms are the entities that represent every emotion or thought that you have ever experienced in your life. In the astral plane, those emotions and thoughts exist in the abstract form. The thought-forms in the astral plane will automatically behave with the knowledge that has been infused into them by the person they were with. All of the thought-forms that you encounter on the astral plane will fill you with greater strength and a sense of purpose. The people, places, and things that you see in your dreams are all versions of the thought-forms from the astral planes. You will often interact with your own emotions and thoughts. It is vital that you try to always remain in some control of your feelings and thoughts because thought forms will exist in both the physical world and the astral world. Your wayward thoughts and extreme emotions will cause your thought-forms to be entirely out of control.

Seeing Into the Afterlife

Your unique stream of consciousness will continue to live on in the astral plane after you die and leave your physical body behind. This could be your subtle body, your spirit, or some part of your essence that is left behind. The beliefs that you hold when you are on the physical plane will determine the destination that your identity will take after your death. You might go on to one of the astral planes. You might begin your life again after you are born back into the world, having no conscious memory of the experience you had before. The main reason that most people fear death is that we have no idea what will happen to us next. There is no real way to know that there is life beyond the one you are living now. There are reports of people having near-death experiences where they describe the bright light, the softness, and the beautiful colors. But the tunnel at the end of all of this beauty might be nothing more than the hallway that takes you to the end of your existence with nothing beyond that to look forward to.

An atheist will have very different views regarding the end of life than someone who has some sort of religious belief. The atheist does not believe in God. Therefore they also do not believe in Heaven as a destination for life after death. Some people think there is a possibility for reincarnation or the option of continuing in some form on an astral plane. The Buddhists do not believe that the soul moves on after death but that the person themselves will be reincarnated a short time after they die. The Hindus also believe in reincarnation and the passing on of the soul. The ideal of the Christians will depend on the particular denomination that they subscribe to, but overall they believe in God as a reality and Heaven as the place that they will go after they die.

If you believe that you will move on to another plane like the astral plane after you die, then you will have the possibility of meeting the Masters. Also known as the Ascended Masters, they are the spiritually enlightened beings who have moved on from this world, leaving their earthly bodies behind for a spiritual existence. They have completed their life cycles and moved beyond the incarnations offered in the physical realm. They are now able to dwell forever in the highest of the astral planes, the Fifth Dimension. When these people were completing their last incarnation on earth, they were known as Yogi, Guru, Shaman, or Spiritual master. During their previous incarnations, they were able to learn all of the lessons that they needed to learn to move on to that exalted level. They were able to complete the divine plan that was set for them and balance out their karmic balance with enough positive to wipe out the negative they had accumulated in their lives. The Ascended Master is very close to the level of the gods. In their new incarnations, they will act as the teachers for human beings while they are working from the spirit realm. They will attend to the spiritual needs of humans by inspiring and motivating the spiritual growth of those they choose to help. Any human can eventually achieve the rank of Ascended Master by following the path of goodness and gathering positive karma throughout all of their incarnations on earth.

Reincarnation

When a soul leaves the body of the deceased person and moves into the body of a newly born person, then that is an act of reincarnation. It is also known as a rebirth or transmigration. As a religious view of life after death, it means that the spirit or the soul of the human will start a new life in a new form after they die. The belief in reincarnation is taught as part of fact by many of the religions of the Far East like Jainism, Buddhism, Sikhism, and Hinduism. The idea behind reincarnation is that you will enter your new form to be a better person in this unique chance at life. You will try to do better than you did in the previous life. How you lived your last life will determine how you will come back to your new life. People who did not try to act as good, decent people in their previous lives might return as a bug or a weed. People who lived as good people will return to a more pleasant experience than the one they had before. The karma that a person collects during their incarnations will determine what form their new life will take. A person who has collected more negative karma than positive karma throughout their reincarnations will need to keep returning to active life until they achieve karmic balance. Someone with more negative karma has not learned to live a righteous life and let go of their ego.

A person will find salvation after death when they finally learn to live the most moral and ethical incarnation that they can live. The form of salvation that they are looking for is not to be born again, because this level of liberation is the real goal of reincarnation. Coming back endlessly in one form after another is not the way most people want to spend eternity. The ultimate goal of reincarnation is to stop being born again and moving into the astral plane.

CHAPTER 5

Opening Your Third Eye Chakra

The sixth of the seven internal chakras is known as the Third Eye Chakra, located between your physical eyes, directly in the center of your forehead. All of your in-depth knowledge and powers of intuition reside in this chakra. The ability to naturally have and use the sixth sense is born into every one, but most people will lose the ability to use it somewhere during childhood. Small children will see and know things that other people, especially adults, will not be able to see and understand. Little children believe that anything is possible because they have not yet learned the ways of the cynical nature of the world. They believe in everything, so then they will be receptive to everything brought to them by their Third Eye. Adults have mostly lost the ability to use the power that the Third Eye will get because they usually don't believe in what they can't see. Once you open your Third Eye and become more receptive to the forces that are lying dormant inside of you, then you will have the ability to be a fantastic receptor for messages from outside of this physical world.

Developing your Third Eye will bring you a level of spiritual awareness that might be overwhelming if there is not a solid foundation in the five internal chakras that are below the Third Eye. When you have done that, and you have opened the Third eye, then you will be more able to see yourself and the world around you, with the inner knowing we possess. Your Third Eye will affect many things in your life. It will influence whether or not you will meet your goals that are related to your deepest desires. It will help you to balance reason and emotion. It will help you to know whether you are moving forward in life or if you are stagnant. You will have a sense of the bigger picture that life presents to you. And it gives you the ability to form gut feelings that are accurate in their predictions.

All of the chakras have unique things that they will relate to, and these are known as correspondences. With the Third eye Chakra, its Sanskrit name is Ajna, which means 'to perceive.' The corresponding color of the Third Eye is indigo, and its corresponding symbol is a lotus flower with ninety-six petals. The aura layer of the Third Eye is the Celestial Body. It works well with all of the elements, but it mostly prefers light. Its goals are to understand and have a psychic perception, and also to use intuition and imagination. The Third Eye also works well with all of the senses, but it mainly prefers the sense of sight. Its corresponding zodiac signs are Sagittarius and Pisces, and its associated planets are Neptune, Mercury, and Venus. The owl and the butterfly are the animals that are associated with the Third Eye Chakra. It responds well to certain essential oils like patchouli, rosemary, vetiver, basil, and jasmine. It also works well with individual crystals and stones such as opal, sapphire, indigo, rainbow moonstone, and lapis lazuli. For foods that correspond to this chakra, look for colors in blue and purple like blueberries, blackberries, purple sweet potatoes, purple kale, grapes, purple cabbage, and eggplant.

Every chakra has its own emotional and physical areas that it directly corresponds to and directly influences. If your Third Eye Chakra is blocked, then you will most likely struggle to find faith in your purpose in life. You might feel as if you and your efforts are insignificant, or that there is no point in you being here or trying to contribute. You will probably struggle to make meaningful decisions. You may also work with trying to learn new ideas or concepts, and you might feel clumsy or have trouble sleeping. On the physical side, you will feel pain in your sinuses, back, and legs. Your eyes will often hurt or feel uncomfortable, and you may be prone to having headaches, especially migraines.

When your Third Eye is open and well-balanced, you will have the ability to connect to your intuitive wisdom and to see deeply into your soul and heart. You will be able to see how all things and all people are connected, and knowing this will help you navigate your way through life. You will be able to trust your innate intuition, and you will enjoy tremendous benefits from it. You will have a powerful and wealthy spiritual foundation that is supported by your understanding and awareness of the world. Awakening your Third Eye Chakra is the first step in being able to tap into all other forms of psychic awareness.

All things that need to pass to you from the outside world will need to go through your Third Eye. It is the bridge that lies between you and the outside world. When your Third Eye Chakra is opened, it will allow you to see what is real, even if those things are clouded by illusion and drama. If this chakra is feeling unhealthy, then you will find it challenging to learn new skills, use your intuition, recall important facts, or even trust your inner voice. When any of the lower chakras are imbalanced, it will make the Third Eye Chakra imbalanced as well, and this can make you feel more judgmental, introverted, and dismissive toward other people. But even if your Third Eye is not currently open, there are methods for reopening it that will soon enable you to be able to use this important chakra.

Dietary Habits

Besides the purple and blue foods, other dietary habits will affect your third Eye Chakra. Cacao (not cocoa) is full of antioxidants that will improve the blood flow to this chakra. It also likes foods that are rich in Omega-3 fatty acids like avocado, salmon, and walnuts. All fruits, but especially blackberries and blueberries, contain antioxidants and flavonoids that will help to decrease your blood pressure, so that more and better circulation will be available to your Third Eye. Prunes and plums have phenols that fight off the free radicals that can attack the area that hold the Third Eye.

The purple vegetables like purple cabbage, purple onions, purple kale, and eggplant carry a variety of different polyphenols that help to reduce inflammation in your body. Inflammation will hinder the flow of blood and oxygen to the Third Eye. While flaxseed, fish, and nuts aren't purple, they do contain Omega-3 fatty acids that will help to lower the risk that you might develop depression and dementia, two conditions that will hamper the working of the Third Eye.

Meditation

Meditation has many benefits for your body. It will help you concentrate better, channel your energies more efficiently, and clear the toxins out of your body. It can also help you and your Third Eye to be more self-aware and active so that your level of consciousness will shift into higher states with each session of meditation. This will help you to operate at your fullest capacity by removing worries and anxiety. Meditation is one of the best and easiest methods for activating your Third Eye. It will help to boost your clarity, improve your concentration, and focus on your mind.

Just like any other form of meditation, Third Eye meditation will require you to be present at the moment. You will need to surround yourself with soothing vibrations and sounds while keeping yourself in a calm environment. Begin your session by sitting in a position that you find comfortable, either on the floor or on a chair. While most pictures of people meditating show them sitting cross-legged on a pillow on the floor, you do not need to try to do this if you physically can't. Not everyone was meant to sit on the floor and get back up again! Sitting in a chair or on some other piece of furniture is a perfectly acceptable alternative. The important thing about where and how you are sitting is that you need to sit somewhere that you can sit upright. Your spine needs to be straight and tall. Keep your shoulders relaxed and lay your hands on your knees or softly in your lap. Open yourself to the positive energy by relaxing your face, stomach, and jaw.

Bring your thumb and your index finger together softly and then gently close your eyes. Meditation is a practice of grace and gentleness. Breathe slowly while inhaling and exhaling through your nose. While your eyes are close, try to look upward, in the direction of your Third Eye. Concentrate on this spot while you continue to breathe slowly. Continue breathing and concentrating on the location of your Third Eye until you can detect a light blue or white light that will begin to surround you. As this light starts to cover you, let yourself begin to succumb to its power. This will take you into the area of metaphysical healing, where your concentration will be at its most effective level because it will be at its highest level. While you are in this state, you will want to let go of any bad energies that you are holding. Let your emotions and thoughts go and just focus on maximizing the potential of your Third Eye chakra. Your priority right now is your focus.

Try to hold your meditation for at least ten minutes and preferably more if you can do so. Peaceful music and soft lighting can help you to stay in the reflection. Set some type of timer before you start so that you are not tempted to watch the clock, and you can concentrate on your meditation. End your session of meditation, just put your palms together gently and take a deep, cleansing breath and let it out slowly. Try to do this meditation daily, either first thing in the morning or just before you go to bed.

Affirmations

An affirmation is a positive word or thought that you would say to yourself, silently or out loud, to combat the negative thoughts you might be having. When you recite affirmations every day, you will be able to keep your chakras balanced, especially the Third Eye chakra. You will become healthier every time you repeat your daily affirmations. The Third Eye chakra prefers assertions that correspond to seeing, both physical and emotional sight. Every chakra has certain theme words that trigger its opening, and for the Third Eye chakra, those theme words are 'I see,' 'I envision,' and 'I imagine." Use the theme words for the Third Eye chakra to create the affirmations that are uplifting and positive, to help you open your Third Eye chakra. Here are a few commitments that you can use to get started.

- I look for guidance and wisdom in all situations.
- The guidance that my third Eye gives me is excellent and safe.
- I embrace my new psychic abilities.
- The answers that I will need are inside of me, and I need to look for them.
- I will forgive and release the things of the past.
- I am the source of love for myself.
- I feel that everything is getting better in my world.
- I hear the voice of my soul speaking to me.
- I see my spiritual truth and ability.
- I will use my intuition for my own higher good.
- I know my higher self, and I will see my higher truth.
- My possibilities are unlimited.
- I will create my reality consciously and with insight.
- I will listen to my intuition when it speaks to me.
- My life is developing the way it was meant to.
- I can capture the larger picture of my life.
- I can see past all of the illusion and drama.
- My imagination is highly creative.
- There is a new vision available for my mind.
- I will expand my awareness.

- Every soul has its light, and I can see it.
- I can see the spiritual path I need to take.
- There are new challenges before me, and I can see them.
- I will only dwell in the present.

Yoga

Yoga poses are beneficial for all parts of the body, including the forehead, where the Third Eye is located. Your Third Eye chakra is where you will find all of your intuition, which everyone has, although not everyone has the confidence to trust their intuition. When you learn to trust your intuition, you will need to go beyond the limits of what is logical and literal. You will need to start to trust your usual perception. When you have a feeling of intuition, you have the feeling of being drawn to those things that are good for you, even if your consciousness wants to resist it. When you open your Third Eye, you will be able to reconnect with who you are. You will then have the ability to navigate your physical world with compassion, kindness, and patience for yourself and others.

Practicing yoga will help to open your Third Eye chakra. To begin, you will first spend a few minutes, turning your gaze to look toward your Third Eye. Cosmic consciousness is provided through this gateway to the physical body. Yoga poses will help you to expand your inner knowing so that you will be able to recognize the symbols and signs that pop up along your path that will guide you toward your life's purpose.

Begin your yoga practice with a pose that is known as Downward Facing Dog. On your yoga mat, get down on the floor on your knees and hands. Make sure that you keep your knees directly under your hips, and your palms are on the floor or the mat slightly in front of your shoulders. Breathe out and lift your knees off the floor. When you first come up keep your knees bent just a little bit and your heels off of the floor. Press your tailbone upward toward the ceiling, breathing in while you do this. Then exhale and push your thighs back while your knees go straight, but not locked.

Make your arms straight, but do not lock your elbows. Keep your head between your upper arms, but keep your neck firm, do not let your head dangle. Stay in this pose for ten to thirty seconds before moving on to the next pose.

Now from Downward Facing Dog, you will move directly into a pose that is called Warrior I. While still in the Down Dog position, step your right foot forward and keep your left foot firmly on the floor. Take a deep breath in and stand up to come into the part that is known as Warrior I. Breath out while you place your fingers together behind your back. Breathe deeply in while you bend forward, putting your right shoulder against the inside of your right knee and pull your palms, with the fingers still together, gently up over your head. Let your shoulders, neck, and head stay firm but relaxed.

Let your arms drift back down as you stand up, and then move your right leg around to stand level with your left leg. Keep your legs spread widely apart. You will now move into the pose that is known as Humble Warrior. Keep your hands behind your back with your fingers placed together as before. Then bend to the front at the waist and lift your hands into the air, keeping the fingers together. Then let go of your fingers from behind your back and reach down and grab each of your big toes with your hands, left hand on left toe, and right hand on the right toe. Stay in this pose for ten to thirty seconds and then put your hands on your hips and slowly rise to a standing position. Bring your feet back together and then fold forward and put your hands on the floor, moving back into the Down Dog position.

While you are still in the Down Dog position, move your left foot forward so that it is in between your hands that are on the mat or floor. Do the Warrior sequence on the left side of your body. Then place your left foot back in line with the right foot, keeping your feet spread far apart. Reach to the front with your right hand and put it flat on the ground about two feet in front of your feet, moving into the Wide-Legged Forward Fold. Hold in this position for ten to thirty seconds, and then repeat this on the left side.

Keep practicing with your yoga positions and work to learn new ones. You can do yoga yourself by yourself at home by watching videos on the television. You can also find a class nearby if that is what you would prefer.

Sound Frequency

There is a unique corresponding frequency for each of the seven internal chakras. Each of the chakras will vibrate at its frequency, and you can learn how to manipulate and influence the frequencies of the chakras so that you can open and balance them and keep them healthy. You are loaded with numerous different frequencies, since every cell in your body has the unique frequency that it will vibrate at. To heal your chakras by using sound frequency, you will need to find sounds on the same frequency as the chakra that you are trying to heal. Once you find the appropriate sound, you will just need to spend some time listening to it while you relax and let the sound frequency do its work. All sound levels are measured in Hz, which is the abbreviation for hertz unit. One hertz unit is equal to one unit of the frequency of the sound. One hertz unit is one vibration, or cycle, of the sound in a second.

Your Third Eye Chakra prefers a frequency of 852 Hz. Music and sound that is set to this frequency will help you replace your negative thoughts with positive thoughts. This frequency is ideal for awakening your intuition and inner strength, which are vital when you are opening your Third Eye. This frequency will also help to calm you when you are feeling anxious or nervous. Listening to this music will help you communicate with your higher self and live in harmony with the Universe.

Essential Oils

Essential oils are often used to open and balance the Third Eye chakra. When the right essential oils are used, they will open this chakra to give you clear seeing, spiritual insight, and clarity of thought. On the spiritual level, the Third eye chakra controls your ability to see connections with others and the more profound truth, understand and trust your intuition, and see straight through illusion and drama. On a mental level, this chakra will help you make better decisions, understand symbolic language, think abstractly, and have good memory skills. On the emotional level, your Third Eye will help rid you of nightmares, make you feel powerful in any situation, and keep you free from delusional thinking. On the physical level, you will enjoy a healthier brain, eyes, and pituitary and pineal gland.

Essential oils will embody the healing properties and frequencies of the plants they came from. These properties and frequencies will work on all types of living beings.

Lavender works to calm your strong emotions and release the pent up energy that your body is holding in. This essential oil will allow for all of the forces of life to flow freely through your body. This oil will allow peace and calm to arise during sleep or meditation, helping you to connect with the astral spirits and the Divine.

Geranium is one of the most valuable essential oils for circulatory issues. It will stimulate the circulation in your brain, and it will also enhance the flow of blood to your pituitary and pineal glands. Geranium can relax and calm your nervous system, and it will help strengthen the vital energy in your body. It is also good to use for those people who spend too much time relying on the left side of their brain. The essential oil of geranium works to bridge the gap between the right mind and the left brain hemispheres to bring to you precise abilities to see well and a more balanced perspective.

Orange Blossom made into an essential oil, which is also known as neroli, is both a tonic and a sedative, and it will work to regulate the function of your nervous system. Neroli has a delicate and sweet citrusy, floral scent. It is often utilized as a natural remedy for shock, depression, and anxiety. Neroli will help to bring more equilibrium to both your mind and your heart, as it is sufficient for both of these centers of energy.

Clary Sage has been used for centuries to treat diseases of the eye. As an essential oil it will help to calm your mind and is especially suitable for treating headaches, especially migraines. Clary Sage essential oil is also used for treating seizures and in the management of epilepsy and autism.

Rose essential oil has a relaxing and calming effect, and it also has the highest vibrational frequency of all of the essential oils. Its high level of vibration makes it ideal for helping to align your physical body with your subtle body to create harmony and balance. This oil will also create an inner sense of well-being while it elevates and stimulates your mind.

Chamomile essential oil will allow you to see the impulses and drives of your ego while it works to soothe and calm your nervous system. It will help you to understand that your projections and purposes, and the various patterns of your ego, are not who you are inside. It will help you see your ego from another perspective and begin to remove yourself from it. This is one of the skills that are vital for you to be able to open your Third Eye.

Melissa essential oil will allow you to access higher vibrations and higher realms while you get in touch with extraordinary realities. It helps to stimulate your pineal gland.

Carrot Seed made into an essential oil is one of the most important of the essential oils that are used on the Third Eye. It has been utilized for centuries to treat diseases of the physical eye. This oil is one essential oil that will allow you to see the reality of the here and now, while it helps you to remain grounded in that reality. It helps to harmonize your physical body with your subtle body. With this harmony, you will be able to experience spiritual insights and visions while staying present in this plane of material existence.

Palo Santo, made into an essential oil, is also known as Holy Wood, and it is used in ceremonies for purification. This essential oil is burned for cleansing auras and as incense. You will use Palo Santo essential oil while you are praying, meditating, or conducting a cleansing ritual. It will enhance your ability to perceive other realms, and it will also heighten your connection to the Divine and your spiritual awareness. It has a rich and sweet aroma

Jasmine essential oil is known in India as the Queen of the Night. It is often used in rituals for healing and magic, and it is associated with the moon. Since the aroma of this essential oil is incredibly uplifting, it will allow you to gain access to the deepest layers of your soul and to deal with the emotional pain that you have repressed there. Jasmine enhances your connection to the Universe and your powers of intuition. While it is compelling for stimulating your senses, it has a sweetly floral aroma.

Bay Laurel that is made into an essential oil is one of the classic essential oils, and it is used to open your doors of perception and heighten your awareness. When you use Bay Laurel essential oil, your powers of clairaudience, clairvoyance, and clairsentience will all be amplified and enhanced. The ancient Greeks liked to use Bay Laurel to increase a seer's ability for prophecy and divination. Bay Laurel essential oil will give you an awakened awareness and a more holistic perception by helping to connect your creative right brain and your rational left brain.

If you are using essential oil to open your Third Eye, one of the best ways to do this is to apply a few drops of the oil to the area where the chakra is so that you would put a few drops in the middle of your forehead. Essential oil is too concentrated, and therefore too strong, to be put directly on your skin. It will need to be added to a carrier oil like baby oil before you place it on your skin. There are varied and exciting ways in which you can use essential oils in your daily life.

- In a small spray bottle of water, put a few drops of the essential oil and use it to spray around your room.
- Use a diffuser to add a few drops to and let the scent fill the room.
- Place five to seven drops of your favorite essential oil on a tissue or a ball of cotton and place it in a bowl next to you.
- Drop a few drops of essential oil into a cup of boiling water for the aroma.
- Mix ten to twelve drops of your chosen essential oil into vegetable oil and then add this to a hot bath.
- Blend six to twelve drops of essential oil into an unscented face or body lotion.
- Place a few drops of essential oil on a tissue and slip it inside of your pillowcase just before going to bed.

Crystals

Using the healing power of crystals is another way that you can use to open your Third Eye. It is effortless to use crystals in your daily life.

- Lie flat on your back and set the crystal of your choice in the middle of your forehead while you meditate or say or think affirmations.
- Hold the crystal in your hand and stare at it while you meditate or say affirmations.

- Set the crystals on the side of the bathtub while you bathe, or drop them into the water.
- Decorate your home or office with various Third Eye friendly crystals.
- Wear jewelry made of the crystals of your choice.
- Carry a crystal or two in your purse or pocket.

Several different crystals will be your best choices for opening your Third Eye.

Amethyst crystal is also called the stone of spirituality. It is a beautiful purple stone that will awaken your mind while it is calming your soul. This crystal will help to open your psychic abilities and help to lift you to the next level of spiritual development by reminding you that you are one with the Divine. The powerful spiritual energies that this stone emits make it the most popular and most common stone for soothing and opening the Third Eye. Amethyst will help to bring balance and harmony when your Third Eye is out of balance. It will aid in strengthening your psychic abilities by bringing clarity to your mind. You can also use a piece of amethyst if you need to heal disorders of your nervous system or your brain, as well as problems with addiction. Amethyst will also calm your stress and frustration as it works to calm your mind. It will allow you to have a more mindful session of meditation. It will also help you recall your dreams and encourage astral travel. Amethyst will give you the patience and wisdom to understand your abilities, and it will help you avoid having nightmares and other negative dreams.

Clear Quartz is often called the master healer of stones because it can be used as a substitute for any rock or crystal of any color. This stone is the only one that you can use on all seven of your internal chakras. The primary purpose of clear quartz is to charge other crystals with its vibrational energies. It will help you awaken your inner abilities by doubling the strengths of all stones you use with it. Your powers of thought and your intentions that you put out to the Universe will be much stronger when you use a clear quartz crystal. The Universe will be able to hear you clearly so that it can assist you. It will also act as your teacher and guide while you are on your spiritual journey, helping you to stay straight on the path to enlightenment. Clear quartz is also a powerful form of psychic protection. When you carry a piece of clear quartz with you or wear it as jewelry, you will be protecting yourself from the negative energies that other people put off. The clear quartz crystal will also help you reduce your negative emotions like ill thoughts, envy, and jealousy.

Labradorite is a very highly protective and spiritual stone that will enhance your psychic abilities when your Third Eye is awakened. It will also shield you from any negative energies and influences and protect your aura from intrusion. This stone is a favorite for psychics and empaths, and since most psychics are empaths, this might be the perfect crystal for you to use. Sometimes referred to as the stone of transformation, labradorite is a highly supportive stone. It will work with your Third Eye to give you a clearer understanding of the intuitive purposes of the struggles and challenges that you might face in life. When you are meditating, labradorite will bring balance into your intuition and intellect. It will also work with your vibrational energies to improve your abilities to discern the truth in all matters. It will also help to regulate your metabolism as well as helping to relieve illnesses of your brain and your eyes.

Lapis lazuli stone has been used and revered since ancient times. This dark blue stone is thought to be the stone of enlightenment and illumination, which makes it a perfect crystal to use with your Third Eye chakra. The flecks of gold in the dark blue stone remind many people of the idea that the night sky is infinite and possible for everything. This stone will help you along the way during your psychic journey. The blue color of the stone will help you detach your consciousness from this realm, and it will help you to open your mind. And this stone is a courageous protector, which it does by using its vibrational energy to connect your mind to the pathways of the soul stars. This will give your mind a form of mental transit along the way, which will help to bind you to the stars and the heavens. And lapis lazuli will work to condition your energy to a higher level of vibrations so that you will be able to improve your progress in spiritual matters. It will work to connect you with the spirit guides and enhance your ability to recall your dreams.

Moldavite is one stone that will work with all seven of your internal chakras, but it works best with the Third Eye chakra. It is quite useful for enhancing your metaphysical abilities. Moldavite will suffice to clear the blockages that are keeping your Third Eye closed, to give it the correct function. This functionality will include spiritual awakening, increased synchronicity, more vivid dreams, and a deeper meaning in your life. Moldavite will also encourage you to be open to new perceptions in your life. It will enhance the flow of energy to your body and mind and help to bridge the gap between the two. Moldavite does work quickly and intensely, so it will need to be used with caution.

Sodalite is a calming stone that will silence the chaotic and negative thoughts that keep you distracted so that your mind will remain calm. While the blue hues, if the stone works to calm your mind, the white veining in the stone will help to align your mind to your higher self, allowing you to begin your psychic journey quickly. This crystal is highly spiritual, and it will work to clear away hallucinations and other mental debris that block the information pathways in your mind. It will enhance your intuitive and spiritual perception. Sodalite also works to rebuild your self-esteem and self-trust and helps you to have a healthy emotional balance in your life by removing your fear and guilt. Sodalite also rejects negativity and seeks the truth in all matters, which will allow you to defend the things that you believe in and always be true to yourself. It will help you to balance your thoughts and feelings.

Moonstone helps you to reconnect to the psychic abilities that you have shut down because of fear and misunderstanding. Moonstone holds the ultimate power of the moon, so it is even more potent at night. It will also keep you well protected at night, especially when you are traveling. The stone will help you to regulate your internal body clock and also work to absorb the negativities and tensions that you collect from your surroundings. Since much of the energy in moonstone is feminine, it is particularly recommended for women to use.

Iolite gives off an energy that heightens your sixth sense and increases your inner vision. It will work on your Third Eye to activate it as well as balance and heal it. Iolite is gentle but powerful enough to help you recognize destructive patterns in your life. This crystal will let you release any of your controlling or domineering tendencies. If you relax with iolite sitting directly on your Third Eye, it will enhance your self-confidence and self-trust while opening up your psychic abilities. It will also assist you in possessing greater mental clarity.

Other Methods for Opening Your Third Eye

There are also other methods for opening your Third Eye. Some of them are listed here:
- Explore new ideas and beliefs that are outside your comfort zone. When your Third Eye is closed, it prefers to be oblivious to the world around it.

- Stop your consumption of processed foods and junk foods. Your body was not made to digest the amounts of sugar, carbs, and fat that are in the typical Western diet.
- Spend some quiet time meditating with a cup of tea made from one of the herbs that support the health of your Third Eye. Some of these include passionflower, rosemary, Ginkgo Biloba, and Gotu Kola.
- Practice mindfulness. Overthinking is one of the symptoms of a Third Eye that is not functioning correctly. Try to keep your thoughts grounded in the present and in the place where you are.
- Take some time to explore your own core beliefs. Sometimes our thoughts and opinions are the cause of a closed or unhealthy Third eye. Make sure that your views are not keeping you locked in a restrictive mindset that is preventing your Third Eye from opening.
- Write your feelings down in a journal. The Third Eye is much attuned to emotions, especially positive ones. Writing them down will help you to become more comfortable with your thoughts and beliefs.

Anyone can open their Third Eye if they genuinely want to. It will take dedication, and you will need to have the willingness to dig into your soul and bring up things you might prefer never to see again. This dedication will help you make the changes that are needed in your life so that you can open and utilize the power of your Third Eye. You will find that the effort is worth it, and you will receive an abundance of mental clarity that will serve you for the remainder of your life.

CHAPTER 6

The Pineal Gland And The Third Eye

In your brain, there is a small endocrine gland that is known as the pineal gland. This gland is the gland that is responsible for the production of the hormone melatonin, which is the hormone that is responsible for putting you to sleep when it is time to go to sleep. This gland is shaped like a little pine cone, which is where it got its name. You will find this gland very near the center of your brain, in between the left hemisphere and the right hemisphere. The melatonin that is created by the pineal gland had many essential functions for the central nervous system. It's most important function is to regulate patterns of sleep, since the production of melatonin is inhibited by light and stimulated by darkness.

While the total role of the pineal gland is still not understood, the ancient traditions and cultures of the world already had an understanding of this gland and its importance. In Taoism, the pineal gland was considered to be the eye of heaven and the eye of the mind. The pineal gland was the seat of clairvoyance and intuition for the ancient Hindus. And the Buddhists referred to the pineal gland as the symbol of spiritual awakening. There were numerous references to the pineal region and the Third Eye in the writings of the ancient Egyptians. The ancient Greeks felt that the pineal gland was the direct connection to thought. They thought the pineal gland was the connecting link between the psychic dimension and the physical world. They referred to the pineal gland as the Third Eye for a straightforward reason. In early versions of autopsies, when the pineal gland was dissected, it was found to be filled with structures that looked precisely like the cones and rods in the retina of the human eye. They understood that light, like sunlight, would flow through the skulls of smaller creatures like fish and birds, and this light would stimulate the pineal gland. The opinion was that the same effect happened in the brains of humans, so the pineal gland became known as the Seeing Eye inside of the mind. They believed that humans would receive messages along with the light directly into the pineal gland.

The pineal gland was once believed to be directly related to the Third Eye Chakra, and it was a useful tool that was revered by the ancient seers and mystics. Much of this power has been lost in the past few centuries as people have stopped tapping into the energy that flows between the pineal gland and the Third Eye. Most people will know that they are not living up to their fullest potential. Even knowing this, most of this knowledge is in the subconscious. This means that you might realize that you are not living up to your full potential, but you don't connect your shortcomings to the reality of the situation. But you do know the difference between the two facts. There are reasons why humans don't operate at the top of their inner power. The human mind doesn't always function the way it is supposed to. Like many other glands, the pineal gland does not work the way it was intended to. You possess the power to change that if you simply follow a few essential steps.

Decalcify and Detox the Pineal Gland

Unlike the rest of your brain, the pineal gland is not isolated by the blood and brain barrier from the rest of the body. The pineal gland gets a large amount of blood flow, with its blood flow being second only to your kidneys. Over time the pineal gland begins to collect calcium deposits from the environment, the foods you eat, and the things that you drink. This causes your pineal gland to slow down in its function of creating melatonin. Then it will stop following your circadian rhythms, and you will find it difficult to sleep at night and stay awake in the daytime.

Poor sleep habits will reduce your mental performance and damage your cognitive function. You can also be more prone to developing diseases. Since the pineal gland is the connection for your body to the natural world, disconnecting it will cause people to be disconnected from each other, the rest of the world, and their instincts. If your pineal gland is not functioning completely, you will make poor decisions and fall prey to false messages and belief systems. When your pineal gland is calcified, you will lose most or all of your tremendous potential. You will need to decalcify your pineal gland to begin the process of your reawakening.

You will need to do three things to decalcify your pineal gland. You will first need to eliminate the environmental causes and the foods that cause calcification in your pineal gland. Then you will need to remove the calcification that is already built up. There are many different ways to do this, and most of them involve using certain supplements to boost your body systems. Then you will need to keep yourself in an environment that will keep your pineal gland healthy and functioning.

Restore your Circadian Rhythm

Some people like to think that the less time they spend sleeping will leave them more time for being productive, but the exact opposite is true. Those people who know the value of a night of good sleep and regularly get the amount of sleep that they need will be much more productive than those people who struggle to stay awake. You can increase your physical energy, expand your cognitive capacities, enhance the power of your memory, and upgrade your mental performance. Still, without the proper amount of sleep each night, none of these methods will work for you.

Your circadian rhythm is the twenty-four-hour cycle of all of the biological activities that are linked to the natural periods of darkness and light. Another term for circadian rhythm is your biological clock. Your physical light meter is your pineal gland. It creates and secretes the hormone melatonin, the hormone that is responsible for the regulation of your circadian rhythm. The exposure of light to your open eyes is the trigger that tells your body how much melatonin to make. Your pineal gland will increase its production of melatonin during the darkness of night, and it will decrease its production during the daylight hours. Melatonin does more in your body than just regulate your circadian rhythm. It also promotes proper healing of damaged tissues, supports the immune response of your cells, works as an anti-inflammatory agent in your body, helps to reduce chronic levels of pain in your body, and it helps you sleep.

Before the use of artificial light, people went outside during the day and stayed inside when it was dark, and the pineal gland knew how to function correctly. The sun was the primary source of light for most people. When people worked under the natural time clock that the sun and the moon provided, their bodies were able to stay in alignment with their circadian rhythms. Now that the world is ruled by artificial light, the pineal gland has lost most of its natural ability to function. And your sleep will suffer because of it.

So while you will probably not be able to ditch all of the artificial light in your own life, there are things you can do to minimize its use and help you get back to a more natural world of light.

Lower the brightness on all of your computer screens as far as you possibly can. During the day, go outside every few hours and look up at the sky, don't look directly at the sun. Take a break from staring at electronics whenever you can. And when it is time to go to sleep, make the room as dark as you possibly can. Even a small bit of light will confuse your pineal gland into thinking it is time to stop producing melatonin, and this will disrupt your ability to fall asleep and stay asleep.

Activate the Pineal Gland

Once you have decalcified and detoxed your pineal gland, and restored your circadian rhythms, then you will need to reactivate your pineal gland so that it will be fully ready to work when you have opened your Third Eye. You are responsible for your journey to higher development and awakening. Follow these steps to activate your pineal gland fully.

The most traditional way to reactivate your pineal gland is by using meditation. Your pineal gland is quite sensitive to the bioelectrical energy signals of dark and light in the environment. You can use meditation to activate this form of energy and direct it to the pineal gland so that you can stimulate it and help it to open fully. A proper meditation for your pineal gland is effortless. Sit somewhere that you are comfortable and relaxed and close your eyes. Focus steadily on your breath and notice how your breath slows just because you are paying attention to it. Once your breathing has slowed, then focus your attention on the area where your Third Eye belongs. Do not try to force your breath and your mind to relax because that will only make you more energetic. Just sit calmly and relax as much as possible. If you expect or want a specific result, you will only succeed in blocking the very energy you wish to entice.

This meditation works because you are focusing your internal energy on your pineal gland and not waiting for something from an outside source. The relaxed focus you adopt will let you sink deeper into relaxation and the stimulation of the pineal gland. Meditating is another way to cause the pineal gland to secrete melatonin. When you begin to feel slight pressure or a pulsing sensation in the area between your Third Eye and your pineal gland, then you will know the meditation is working.

While you have probably been told all of your life that staring directly at the sun is dangerous, when you do it for short periods, it is beneficial. If you are genuinely committed to the idea of tapping into your higher potential, then you will need to be ready to question everything that you think you now know. You will find that most of the things that you have learned are somewhat limited in their scope, or are false. Staring at the sun directly, or sun gazing, is one of these things. It is an ancient technique that will offer you powerful benefits. The theory behind the practice is that you will absorb the energy of the sun directly through your skin and eyes.

The safest time for you to practice sun gazing is early in the morning, as the sun is beginning to rise because the sun will be closer to earth at that time and will not be as strong. Stand barefoot so that you are in touch with the ground, and do not look through a window; you need to be outside to do this. Begin with looking at the sun for just ten seconds at a time and slowly build your tolerance for up to thirty minutes. You can partially close your eyes if you feel the sun is too bright. If the day is cloudy, then stare at the spot in the clouds that is in front of the sun. The theory behind this technique is that the sun is the force of life for all things, and by staring directly at the sun; you will collect large amounts of energy for your pineal gland and Third Eye.

Sungazing might also help you with another method for activating your pineal gland, and that method is fasting. People who regularly sun gaze report that they feel less hunger, and they find that fasting is easier for them. Periodic fasting is right for your body in so many ways. It will increase your levels of human growth hormone, which helps your body regenerate, and it will help lower your risk of developing many chronic diseases. There are many different schedules that you can follow if you would like to give intermittent fasting a try. Fasting will also help to detoxify your body, which will help to reactivate your pineal gland.

Practicing the ancient art of Qigong (chee-gong) is another method for reactivating your pineal gland. The exercises serve to increase the flow of energy through your body and your sensitivity to that energy. You will learn how to move the energy around in your body by using breathing and gentle motions. Then you can move this energy with intent by using just the power of your mind. Most people have blocked energy channels that prevent the energy of life to flow freely through their bodies. These blockages prevent the fuel from reaching the parts of your body where it is most needed. When the energy can flow freely, it can get all aspects of the body, including the pineal gland.

When you think about activating your pineal gland, you are talking about bringing all of the power in your mind to actualization. This power will allow you to use all of the parts of your mind together. Once you have reactivated your pineal gland and you can open your Third Eye, a whole new world will open up for you. You will begin to perceive your reality quite differently. You will start to notice more of your unconscious behavior. This process will alert you to many new facts about your own life and the Universe around you. You will learn many truths about life itself that you were not able to know before. This path is a new adventure for you, and the door is always open.

CHAPTER 7

Reiki Healing And The Third Eye

Reiki healing uses energy to heal the physical body and the subtle body. Reiki healers use the palms of their hands to lie on the patient in a technique known as palm healing. The word Reiki is derived from two words that mean divine vitality. The theory behind reiki is that the practitioner can bring down the dynamism of the divine by using themselves as the medium and their hands as the instrument. It is a subtle method of guiding your life force using the energy from the divine and the Universe.

All the energy that flows through all living beings is the force of Reiki. Healers will practice with the intention that all people hold within them the ability to heal themselves if they can connect with the appropriate healing energy. This energy is in you, and you can use it to heal yourself and other people. It would help if you had your power to be healthy and flowing freely through your body. When your energy flows freely, then your mind and body will vibrate positively with good health and strength. When your life is blocked or stagnant, then you will experience physical or emotional imbalances.

Reiki as a healing practice has been used since the late nineteenth century. Japanese monks used the techniques and taught them in their monasteries. Several different forms of Asian healing techniques provided the specific methods and techniques of Reiki. The basic concept is that imbalances of energy cause disease, and the body will heal itself when these imbalances are corrected. The idea is finding favor in the West and is widely used in Eastern medicine even today.

Modern practitioners use the same techniques that were taught centuries ago by the monks. The ancient concept of an infinite supply of energy for healing the body still rings true with Reiki healers. Those who have mastered the Reiki technique will use attunements, which is a process to teach others how to master Reiki themselves. During a session, the patient will lie down on a table, and the master will let their hands hover over the patient. Energy will flow through the master and down into the patient. Illness or injury will show in the patient where the power is blocked. The master will lay their hands over the blockage to allow the healing energy to release the jam.

Reiki will improve symptoms and conditions like insomnia, tension, headaches, and nausea. It will help to relieve your anxiety and depression, so it works to improve your mood. It can improve your self-confidence and self-esteem. You will be able to relax with better sleep patterns, and this will provide you with calm nerves and inner peace. Relieving your physical symptoms will help your emotional symptoms to improve. People with severe or chronic illnesses will enjoy relief from pain, anxiety, and fatigue.

Some masters will use crystals to make the Reiki session more powerful. They will place these crystals around your body, or on different points of your body, to let the energy from the crystals enhance the energy from the Reiki session. Some of the crystals more commonly used are rose quartz, amethyst, moonstone, topaz, tourmaline, and aquamarine.

Reiki is effective when used to heal the Third Eye chakra. Your entire body will benefit from the energy that is released when the Third Eye is healed. Your Third Eye has an important role in balancing your inner vision and emotional peace. The practitioner will use the Reiki techniques to release the blockage that is hampering the function of your Third Eye. Reiki also helps your mind be receptive to the energy of the divine that will flow to you through the Third Eye. Your mental state will greatly improve during the session, because your body will relax and your mind will cease activity. This will give you inner peace, and that will help you gain the perfect state that will allow the spirits to come to you. Once your Third Eye is opened then the energy of the Universe will flow through it to reside in you.

CHAPTER 8

Psychic Abilities And Your Third Eye

Now that your Third Eye is awakened to the possibilities of life, you will be able to take advantage of all of the new psychic abilities that will be available to you. People with psychic powers are nothing more than regular individuals who possess the abilities that go beyond the boundaries of the material world. These people can sense, feel, taste, hear, and see, and they have the power of intuition. Psychic skills are the ability to process the data that you receive from intangible and tangible stimuli on a profoundly physical, spiritual, or emotional level. Psychic abilities vary significantly in application and intensity.

Most psychic abilities are developed originally in childhood. Children see more, feel more, hear more, and notice more. Children are naturally more psychic because they believe everything is real, even spirits. When children grow older and are steered more in the direction of math and science and less in the way of imagination and creativity, they will lose their psychic abilities. Adults accept that the physical world is the only realm that exists. But your psychic skills are never lost, and you can quickly revive them with a little practice.

Mahamudra Meditation

This meditation style is a form of highly intentional meditation that will help you realize your full potential after you have opened your Third Eye. The true nature of your abilities will not come from accidents, good luck, or willpower. Psychic skills need to be worked on, and this is where you can use Mahamudra meditation to hone your abilities. You can use this knowledge to do your practice for psychic openness. You will need to begin with understanding what this form of meditation is. There are three distinct parts to Mahamudra meditation. It starts with Ground Mahamudra, which will show you how to find the fundamental reality in your world and your mind. Path Mahamudra will teach you how to start on your practice of this form of meditation. Fruition Mahamudra shows where the path of this meditation will take you. When you have learned to work through all three parts, then you will experience the total picture of your journey of awakening that is known as Mahamudra.

Your mind is spacious, open, and transparent, and you will see this with a clear and steady focus after learning this meditation. In the beginning, you will not be able to see and enjoy your thoughts and emotions, as they will vaporize when you focus on them. There is wisdom in emptiness, and you will need to learn to recognize and accept this emptiness to realize your true potential. Your mind will be awakened and will become aware of the wisdom that the void allows inside. You must be able to empty your mind so that you can accept the knowledge of the divine after your Third Eye is open. This wisdom is what will bring you true enlightenment. Opening your Third Eye is just the first step. It is like opening the door to a house. Once the door is open, then people and things can come in, but the door must first be opened. This reality is what opening the Third Eye will do for you. It is just a means to an end, one step on the path to true enlightenment.

You will need to become familiar with how your mind will work now so that you can learn how to use it correctly, and this is what Mahamudra meditation will teach you. Your first glance into your mind will reveal a space where thoughts are poorly organized, and they are allowed to wander in all directions. Your mind will need guidance so that it will work correctly. Your first learning will be methods for bringing order and clarity to your mind and your thoughts. When you are mindful of the workings of your thought processes, then your awareness will become more precise and sharper. As your mind learns how to relax and expand, then you will inhabit a dimension open in the present. Mahamudra meditation will show you how to rest within the nature and openness of your mind and how to see clearly for the first time. With most reflections, you need to concentrate on an object or a thought, focusing your attention on one thing. Mahamudra meditation allows your mind to relax and clear itself in a natural state. The best description of this form of meditation is learning to release stress and relax while being mindful of the present. Although this kind of meditation might feel unnatural and stressful in the beginning, as you practice, you will become more comfortable with the techniques.

Find a place that is free of distractions and sit down and relax. Focus on how good it feels to sit there and relax. Feel your thoughts and your breath. Take as long as you need to sit quietly and relax, breathing slowly and deeply. Look directly in front of you with focus, letting your eyes see what is there and your mind understand what is there. Then gradually allow your vision to become unfocused so that you are looking more at the whole area in front of you but focused on nothing in particular. Quietly relax in this position for a few minutes. Accept without judgment or comment any emotions, thoughts, or feelings that come into your mind. It is normal for your mind to try to fill itself. The opinions and feelings are neither bad nor good; they are. Let your mind relax and accept what comes.

The object of this form of meditation is to focus on the clarity, emptiness, and awareness of your mind as it learns to relax and be receptive. You will understand the true nature of your mind while you are unfocused and open. Reflect on the space in your mind and the openness that lies within, while you are allowing your mind to be empty. You will gain clarity from the radiance that fills your mind. Sit calmly and star into space while your mind rests and becomes calm. Think of the new clarity in your mind. See and feel the emotions and thoughts that are nothing more than the natural expressions of an open mind. Acknowledge your thoughts, but do not let yourself feel them. A happy idea will not bring happiness, and an angry view will not bring anger. You are more concerned with not judging your thoughts than you are about having the thoughts. This acceptance will bring you awareness of the mind. Relax in the clarity of your mind while you stare into the space in front of you. Gradually let your eyes begin to refocus, and your mind comes back into the present. Sit quietly for a few more minutes before you go about your daily activities.

Writing Automatically

When you are in an altered mental state such as a trance, you may be able to indulge in automatic writing. The ability to do this comes from a place that is outside of your conscious awareness, most often from another astral plane. Automatic writing might be the inner workings of your mind, or it might be the messages that you receive from spirits and angels through your Third Eye. It might also be the work of your subconscious relating to your subtle body or your higher self.

Working to perfect your automatic writing abilities will help you reap numerous benefits. You will develop a deeper trust in your instincts and intuition. You will feel supported and deeply understood. You will make contact with the spirit guides assigned to you so that you can know their perspectives and opinions. Your decisions will be smarter, and your intuition will be sharpened and better developed. And since you will have the ability to receive direction from higher powers, your daily life will be filled with clarity and precision.

Automatic writing will calm you while it works to open your mind. It is simple to execute and can be done anytime. Have your paper and pen ready when you sit down to relax, so you are prepared to write your responses. Think of a question that needs answering or a problem that you are experiencing. Write your question on the top of the paper. Now sit back and relax, opening your mind while you think of the item that you wrote down. Remain utterly relaxed in mind and body while you wait for answers. As the feelings and thoughts begin to come to you, let your writing flow freely onto the paper. Do not worry about grammar or syntax, but let the ideas flow from your mind, through your arm and hand, and down onto the paper. Do not proofread your work or add punctuation. Your writing may not make sense to anyone but you, but that is not what is essential. The critical part of this exercise is for you to become comfortable with receiving messages from the spirit world, and then letting those messages become thoughts that you can freely express through your writing. This is not a skill that you will immediately excel with. Automatic writing takes time and patience to develop, so do not be discouraged if your first few attempts do not give you the results you were hoping to have. Just keep following the steps, and soon you will be an expert at automatic writing.

When you form your question, make sure it is something that you need help with and not just a random thought. This technique might be the outlet you need, especially if you are struggling to receive messages through your newly opened Third Eye. Meditate before you begin your session if you need to so that your mind will be open and receptive. Make your question vital to you, since you will receive a better response if there is thought and emotion involved in the question. Choose the specific entity from which you want a reply. You can query your subtle body, your subconscious mind, a spirit guide, or the divine. It will be easier for them to form an answer if your question is simple. You will need to keep your session to just one problem, performing more sessions if you have more than one problem.

Let your mind relax fully before you begin. This relaxation is where the meditation will help you the most. You might find that this is the most challenging step since life today is so crazy sometimes. But it is vital that your mind is relaxed and clear when you begin. If your mind is cloudy or cluttered, you might not receive the exact messages you need. Any method will work to clear your mind if meditation does not work for you. Try using crystals or essential oils, or do a few yoga poses. Mindfulness and deep breathing might also help you.

Enter a light trance as you begin your session. A trance is a form of altered consciousness that is relatively easy to attain. It will allow your mind to relax fully. Your automatic writing will flow more quickly if your mind is relaxed. If you find it challenging to enter a trance, you can try some guided meditation or self-hypnosis. You can also enter a trance by listening to soft music, repeating a chant or mantra, or doing repetitive tasks.

Once you have entered your trance and the information is coming to you, do not try to stop it. As soon as you are ready, you can begin writing. It is okay if the words you write make no sense. Writing nonsense words is a good sign because it means that you have tapped into a flow of information that is outside of your conscious mind. If your conscious mind tries to intrude, ease it back into the trance. You might need to spend a few minutes getting back into your trance, and this is normal in the beginning. Just remain relaxed, and it will come back to you quickly. You might also need to adjust to the practice of writing, mostly if you usually text or type everything. Take the time to practice your automatic writing, and you will naturally improve.

Wait until the information stops flowing to you before you try to read what you have written. It will be easy for you to know when your session is over. The thoughts and feelings will stop coming to you, or your writing will just stop. When that happens, you can take the time to analyze what you have written. First, look for any phrases or words that make sense. Pick out any word that you have used more than once. You will not receive your information from simply reading what you have written, because it will not be written clearly in sentences and paragraphs. You will need to put all of the clues together to make sense of what you have written. And if the information you recorded on the paper makes absolutely no sense to you, then that might be the sign that you need to ask a different question or ask your question differently.

If the thoughts you recorded are disjointed and vague, that is a good sign that the ideas are coming from your divine source. When you write frantically, and the words make sense, that is a good sign that you are writing down the emotions in your mind and soul. Automatic writing will flow lightly across the paper, and the words will be nonsensical and a bit garbled. Keep practicing, and you will be able to make automatic writing work for you.

Yoga for your Mind

Once your Third Eye is open, you will begin to receive messages from various sources. Sometimes your messages may come across as harsh or negative thoughts and emotions. When this happens, you probably need to spend some time stretching your mind so that it can continue to learn and grow. When your feelings cross over into your spiritual thoughts, you may need to take advantage of some mental yoga to help clear your mind. Mental yoga does for the mind what physical yoga does for the body. It will help you to stretch your mind and your emotions, clearing out excess toxins and unnecessary feelings and thoughts. Mental yoga might cause you some discomfort, but it will help bring you where you want to be.

Sometimes people think that, because their Third Eye is open and functioning, that their psychic abilities will naturally develop and display themselves on command. This rapid ability rarely happens. There will be some discomfort when you begin this journey, and that is needed for you to grow emotionally and spiritually. Mental yoga is made of three different ideas. You will first need to accept that your emotions are normal and acceptable. They are a natural part of you being human. Life will give you anger, happiness, sadness, and regret over your lifetime, and these are all-natural. You need to accept your emotions so that you can function better mentally and emotionally. Do not try to control your feelings or eliminate them; accept them. Examine your feelings without reacting to them or judging them, and use your natural curiosity to learn from your emotions, especially the negative ones. It is easy to understand why you are happy, but you also need to know why you have negative feelings. Your curiosity will engage your logic, and this will allow you to learn from your reactions to your emotions. Then you can harness that knowledge to create intelligent steps to move closer to your goals. You will find it easier to commit to actions and behaviors that will help you achieve your goals if you are not stressed about your reactions or trying to resist them.

Those people who study the ancient art of yoga as it was meant to be used know that yoga is not just about the poses. The traditional practice of yoga is not just a form of exercise that involves stretching and bending. The real benefit of yoga is the mental, psychological, and spiritual clarity it will give you. Yoga is a way of life with benefits for all areas of your life. The actual practice of yoga will keep you in a healthy frame of mind as it balances your mind as well as your body. Ashtanga yoga is one of the best yoga practices for keeping a clear mind and body. The principles of this discipline will guide you through an enlightened life. Ashtanga yoga is one of the oldest yoga disciplines and one of the most authoritative. Ashtanga yoga has eight different philosophies, called the eight limbs that will guide all aspects of your life. The philosophies deal with cultivating internal awareness, yoga poses, concentration, self-discipline, meditation, integrity, transcending the self, and controlling your breathing. Transcending the self is the eighth limb, and you will need to attain the other seven levels if you want to achieve the eighth one. Practicing Ashtanga yoga will bring you to the level of awareness that you want to accomplish with your newly opened Third eye.

With the first limb, you will focus on your behavior and how you conduct yourself as you travel through life. You will examine your integrity and your ethical standards, as you try to live your life in a manner that will allow you to be kind to others, treating others as you want to be treated. The second limb will teach you to remain spiritual while you learn self-discipline. This spirituality does not mean attending church if that is not your style. You will need to determine what a spiritual practice means to you, and then take care of your spirituality. Even taking a walk alone in the woods can be a spiritual experience. Through your spirituality, you will practice contentment, learning about yourself, surrendering to the divine, being happy with less, and cleanliness.

Next, you will learn the poses that make up the yoga part of the practice in the third limb. In your training, you will discover that your body is your temple and needs to be revered and cared for. The yoga poses will develop your ability to concentrate and your habit of discipline. The fourth limb is controlling your breath, where you will learn different techniques that will teach you how to manage your respiratory processes. You will also learn more about the connection between your emotions and your mind and breath. Proper breathing techniques will not only revive your body, but it will also help you live longer. The first four limbs of Ashtanga yoga deal mainly with you and your body. You will learn to develop an energetic awareness of yourself, gain mastery over your body, and refine your personality. All of this will help prepare you for the second part of your journey and the next four limbs that deal more with the use of your newly opened Third Eye.

When you begin the fifth limb of Ashtanga yoga, you will make a conscious effort to turn inward to your mind. You will draw your awareness away from stimuli from the outside and the wider world. You will direct your attention inward as you become more aware of your senses, even while you are removing your focus from them. You will need to take a few steps back and look at yourself honestly. This self-examination will also allow you to examine any cravings you might have and work to get rid of them since they will interfere with your spiritual growth and ruin your health.

The first five stages have prepared you for the sixth limb, the one of concentration. Now that you have removed the outside distractions from your life, you can begin to deal with all of the distractions inside your mind. Concentration comes before meditation, and it will allow you to slow down your thinking by focusing on a single object. This focus will be a purely mental focus, not on an actual item, and it can be the silent repetition of a sound, an image of the divine, or one of the energy centers in your own body. You have already started to withdraw from your senses by controlling your breathing and developing your ability to concentrate. Now you will focus on a single item and not allow your mind to wander during your practice. When you can focus for long periods of time, this will lead you naturally into meditation.

The seventh limb of Ashtanga yoga is the practice of meditation. This meditation is the uninterrupted flow of your concentration. You will notice a definite line of distinction between concentration and meditation, even though the two work together. Concentration involves focusing on a single thing, while meditation is more concerned with being acutely aware without focusing on any one thing. In this stage, your mind has learned to be quiet and produce few thoughts or none at all. It takes stamina and strength to get to this point. If you do not reach this point right away, keep trying. Yoga is not a goal, it is a practice, and you may need more time to achieve the results you want to achieve.

Once you have traveled through the first seven stages of Ashtanga yoga, you will be ready for the eight steps, the final limb, and the exalted state of ecstasy. When you reach this stage, you will be able to merge with the point you are focusing on and completely transcend yourself. This will give you the connection to the divine you are seeking, and it will show you your connection to the entire Universe. This realization will give you the peace that will surpass all levels of conscious understanding. This aspiration is not a lofty goal or one that makes you better than other people. It is a goal that most people hope to obtain in life, the freedom and fulfillment of achieving their hopes and desires. The completion of the path is the goal of most people, and that goal is internal peace. This peace will give you the enlightenment you need to achieve your self-realization.

Your journey through the eight stages can sometimes be difficult, so be kind to yourself. Some may call this selfishness, but it is just taking care of you. You will not be able to achieve the enlightenment that comes with a functioning Third Eye is you are not prepared physically, mentally, and emotionally. Be honest about how you feel. The purpose of mental yoga is learning to put yourself first so that you are prepared for the demands of life.

Spiritual Beings on Earth

When your Third Eye has awakened and you can receive and send messages with your mind, you will also find that you are more intuitive when it comes to an understanding of other people. This understanding will not only make you more empathetic, but it will allow you to see the spiritual side of other people. Since humans are spirits living in the astral plane known as earth, you will be able to discern the souls who are around you. Everyone who has gone on to another astral plane leaves a part of themselves behind, and you will recognize them through the powers of your Third eye.

Those who are reincarnated after they die will return to earth in another form, usually a human, The idea is that they will need to live again to satisfy some sort of karmic imbalance from their previous life. Sometimes only a part of the soul will come back to earth, and the rest of it will reside on another astral plane. A human spirit can be made up of as many as six parts, and it is not uncommon for the different parts to take turns returning to earth, while the others stay on the astral plane. When they come back together, they will compare experiences and prepare for the next incarnation. When the soul returns to earth, it will bring its spirit guardian. Sometimes that spirit guardian is one of the other parts of the soul from the astral plane.

The guardian spirit comes to earth with the human to watch over them and help protect them. They will also inspire their humans to make the right decisions. The guardian spirit can travel between the human world and the spirit world as they choose. The guardian wants their human to be safe, but also to be happy. You can receive guidance from your spirit guardian by simply acknowledging their presence in your world. When your Third Eye is open, it will be easier for you to receive guidance, and it will be more vital for you to seek advice from your spirit guardian. Opening your Third Eye can be stressful and scary, and your spirit guardian will be able to help you through the changes you will experience calmly. Your spirit guardian will come from one of many different sources.

Guardian angels belong only to you, and they will devote all of their time to taking care of you. They come with you when you are born, and they will leave when you die. The archangel is the leader angel of all of the spirit guides. These spirit guardians are loaded with powerful energy. When you call for assistance from an archangel, you will most likely feel an extra surge of life, especially if you are extra sensitive or you are empathic. Helper angels can help you at any time because they are not attached to anyone human. They work freely and go wherever they are most needed. Any of these spirit guardians can help you relieve the stress that comes from utilizing the power of your Third Eye.

Sometimes the people you have known and loved will come back to be your spirit guardian after they leave earth. Any human who has lived and died can become a spirit guardian, and they will generally seek someone who is similar to themselves in thought and action. If you are struggling with the perceptions from your Third Eye, call on one of these spirit guardians, especially seeking one who had their struggles with Third Eye enlightenment.

Your spirit guardian will not be able to contact you directly until you contact them first. They will send you messages, mainly through Third Eye reception, so you need to be open to receiving these messages. Sometimes they will come to you as feelings or thoughts, and sometimes they will come to you as concrete symbols of a message you are seeking. If you see a self-help book on a day you are feeling particularly needy spiritually or emotionally, then that might be a sign from your spirit guardian. They might send messages to you with numbers you consider to be lucky. They might make you think of a special person when you hear a particular song. Your spirit guardians have many ways to get messages to you, so you need to be receptive to your thoughts and the signs you see.

Methods that you can use to facilitate communication with your spirit guardian will also help you strengthen the powers of your Third Eye. Develop a regular spiritual practice. Send your spirit guardian a specific message. Experiment with divination by using oracle cards, runes, or tarot cards. Hold the item in your hands and ask for guidance from your spirit guardian before you begin. Give your spirit guardian a particular problem that you need help with, and then wait patiently for the answer.

Practice with different methods to improve your clairvoyance. Write about your spirit guardian in a journal. Give your spirit guardian a unique name that no one but you and they would know. And work on being mindful, so that you are mentally and emotionally present and available when your spirit guardian sends messages to you. Your physical eye will tell you everything that you need to know about the physical world, but your Third Eye will give you all the information you need about heavenly matters and your spirit guardian. When your Third Eye is open, you will be able to see beyond the restraints of the physical world, and you will understand your connection to the larger world.

Earth Angels and Advanced Spirits

Some of the spirit guardians are real angels from Heaven who have come to help you. They have important things to do one earth. They will help you open your Third Eye and learn to use it for good purposes. They will help you realize your full potential once your Third Eye is open. Helping you raise your vibrational level so that you can freely send and receive messages through your Third Eye is one of their specialties. Their ultimate goal is to make your ability to communicate with the spirit world stronger.

Angels are compassionate beings who do not tolerate violence or anything that is not real. The Laws of the Universe guide them, and they operate on the principles of love, purity, and trust. Unfortunately, they believe that all people they encounter will feel the same way that they do, so they are often disappointed. If you meet an angel on earth, you will know it, for they are gentle souls who often resemble extensive children. The happiness they carry in their hearts keeps them looking perpetually young. They are unusually sensitive to the energies in the people around them and the vibration that people emit.

The advanced spirits will travel a difficult path while they are on earth. Their job here on earth is to restore harmony, love, and balance to humanity. The spiritual way they walk is one designed to improve the world by making people more in tune with their feelings and thoughts, and open to ideas from the spirit world. They connect with people in a completely selfless manner. All of the entities of the world are open to their guidance, whether that entity is human, animal, or plant. Even if their lives are not ideal, they will always seek their higher purpose in life, and they will work to help you find your higher purpose. They will never react to anyone or anything with anger or bitterness. Advanced spirits will spend all of their time trying to bring out the best in all people. Emanating a magnetic field that draws needy people to them, they have brightly shining lights that make them easy to find.

The Third Eye and Your Aura

Having an open Third Eye will give you the ability to see the aura of other people. Since an aura is created from the colors that will correspond to the energies that come off the other person, reading their aura is almost like looking into their soul. All living people have their aura that surrounds them like a blanket, showing off their real personality to anyone who can read their aura. When your Third eye is open, you will be able to read auras with a little practice. Auras are made of seven separate layers, and each layer corresponds to one of the chakras inside of the person. The aura is the external reflection of the inner subtle body of the person. Those people who have more internal energy will have a more massive aura. Every aura has a unique pattern of blockages and openings that correspond to the internal energy of the person. Once you have developed your powers of clairvoyance, you will easily be able to read auras.

Each aura is made of three distinct planes and seven bodies of energy. The three planes are the physical plane, the spiritual plane, and the astral plane. The physical plane includes your etheric body, your emotional body, and your mental body. The physical plane and the spiritual plane are linked together by the astral plane. The spiritual plane works to connect you to your intuition and the divine. It is your spiritual plane that is the most crucial aspect of your spiritual self and your Third Eye. The different colors in your aura will directly reflect the health of the internal chakras in your body. If any of your chakras are not healthy, that will be displayed in the color and health of your aura. The differences in the colors of the aura will tell how you are feeling mentally, physically, emotionally, and spiritually. Your aura will continue to change colors as the health of your chakras changes. The aura is attached to you with thin attachment cords that hold it to your body. Besides the appearance of the colors, the aura can also show holes and tears if the chakra is damaged.

If you want to be able to read and understand the aura of someone accurately, then you will need to understand what the colors mean. You also need to know where your aura ends, and the aura of the other person starts so that you are not transferring information about your aura to the aura of the person that you are reading. When your Third Eye is well developed, you will easily read an aura by merely glancing at it. It will also help you know the strength of the personality and the spirit of the other person, and be able to tell where they might be suffering a blockage.

Mirrors and Crystal Balls

Scrying is an essential method for divination for anyone who has opened their Third Eye. Mirrors and crystal balls are both used for scrying. Detecting messages of significance or visions is the primary purpose of scrying. You can use scrying for divination. You might be looking for some sort of personal guidance, prophecy, revelation, or inspiration when you are scrying. Crystallomancy, which is the method of using mirrors or crystal balls for scrying, is a form of spiritual work that you will take part in when your Third eye is open. You might want to keep your mirror or your crystal ball in a place of honor, such as on an altar.

When you do a reading, you are seeking to find a visionary sight that will provide you with knowledge about a particular subject. You can do a reading for yourself or someone else. Gazing into the mirror or the crystal ball will reveal psychic visions. Diviners and psychic readers who use mirrors or crystal balls for information will often study stones and crystals to learn more about their traditional knowledge. A stone or crystal can be used in place of a mirror or crystal ball when needed. Some readers will have different types of crystals for various purposes, their crystal ball being the largest one and the one that is most often used. If you choose to use crystals, then you will want to select the ones that have intentions and purposes that match your question. Quartz or calcite will be used when you want to send out blessings to someone, or if you need to see far into the distance either spiritually or physically. A piece of amethyst can let you know if someone is carrying addictions they want to keep hidden. Black obsidian would be used to determine if there is terrible magic working against someone.

Before you perform a reading, you will need to cleanse your mirror or crystal ball. Of course, you would keep it clean, but this type of cleansing has more to do with removing the remnants of past readings and any negative information the crystal ball has retained. You can use water, smoke, or herbs to clean your crystal ball. If you are using water to cleanse the ball, it should not be tap water, but some form of purified water. Rainwater is also a good choice for cleansing purposes. Add sea salt to the water and let the ball soak, fully immersed, for twenty-four hours, then wipe it with a clean white cloth. If you are using herbs, then you will want to smudge the ball. Put the herbs of your choice in a heatproof bowl and ignite them. Sandalwood, frankincense, and sage will work well for this purpose. When the herbs begin to give off smoke, use your hands to guide the smoke to waft over the crystal ball. Then wipe the ball with a clean white cloth. If there is a safe place in your yard, then you can bury the crystal ball for twenty-four hours and let the power of the earth cleanse it.

When you have cleansed your crystal ball, you are ready to perform the reading. If you need to clean the ball first, then do that one full day before the reading. You can perform a reading anywhere, but it is best done in a quiet place that is free of interruptions and distractions. Use herbs or incense to smudge the area where you will do the reading. Layout some crystals around the room to help protect your reading from unwanted intrusions of unrelated messages. Send out to the universe your intention to only invite positive messages and energies to participate in your reading.

Cradle the stone or ball gently in your hands. If you are using a large crystal ball, then you can place it in a holder on the table directly in front of you. When you are close to the sphere, you will make contact with it, and this is needed so that you can connect with its energies, so if you are not holding the crystal ball, then touch it with both hands. Breathe in and out deeply three times, repeating the word 'relax' as you exhale. Continue breathing while you focus on your breaths and let all of your thoughts disappear into the background. Gaze into the crystal ball and hold this gaze for several minutes. Let the messages and visions enter your mind through your Third Eye. Do not concentrate on them or try to force them to appear. You might see simple forms and shapes within the crystal ball, and scenes and images may appear in your mind. The divine may also send messages to you at this time. Depending on your ability and the level of trance you can reach, a reading can last anywhere from a few minutes to several hours.

When you have finished your reading, always remember to thank the divine energies for the wisdom they provided you in this session. Take three deep breaths to stabilize yourself. Come out of the trance slowly and allow your thoughts and energies to realign within you.

The Afterlife and the Third Eye

When you have opened your Third Eye, and you are using its powers to amplify your life, you will be able to communicate with celestial beings and people who have died and left this physical world. When people die, their stream of consciousness, which makes up their energy, will continue to live on in an astral plane. This part of you might be your spirit or your soul, or it might just be a part of your essence that lives on after you are gone. With an open Third eye, you will be able to make contact with these souls and spirits in the astral plane. The eventual landing place of a departed soul will depend on their previous life on earth and their personal beliefs. They might spend eternity in their version of Heaven. They may be reincarnated back into the world. It is believed that those souls who are reincarnated will have no memory of the life they lived before so that you may encounter the same spirit in several different forms throughout your life.

Since everyone will eventually die, it is best to form your own opinion of it and learn to accept the inevitable. With your open Third Eye, you will be able to continue communicating with those who are gone, and with others after you are gone. Part of the fear of death is the absence of knowledge of what happens after you die. There are many theories around life after death, people have reported having near-death experiences, and some people will admit that they have lived before. There are reports of softness, lovely colors, and intensely bright lights that surround the end of the corridor where you are prompted to walk at the end of your life. It is possible that the passage does not lead to the end of your journey but is simply the doorway to the next trip. Christians hold that God does exist, and there is a Heaven, and this is where you want to go when you die. Buddhists do not believe that people have a soul, but they do think that everyone goes on into their new existence shortly after death. Since atheists do not believe in God or Heaven, they do not see this as the eventual destination. Some do believe in reincarnation and life on the astral plane after physical life is ended.

Reincarnation is also known as rebirth or transmigration, depending on the system of beliefs that you hold in your physical life. It is the philosophical or religious belief that your soul or spirit will take on a new life in a new physical form after the original physical body ceases to exist. When you take on your new way of life, the concept is that you will try to live a better life and be a better person than the one you had before. The new form that you take may depend on your behavior in your previous experience. Some people believe that if you were an undesirable person or live a less than desirable life in your last incarnation, then you will return as a less desirable life form in your next embodiment.

The idea behind reincarnation is to allow you to balance your karmic collections by living again when it is needed. As you go through life, you collect karmic impressions that are based on the kind of person you are and the kind of life you lead. People who try to do good things or live good lives will collect more positive karma than negative karma. A soul is not able to leave its physical body forever until its karmic balance is positive, so some people might go through many incarnations before they get the equation right. You will know who these people are on earth, through the power of intuition your Third Eye gives you, and you will be able to help them if you can. You can increase your positive karmic collection if you can help these people, and you do it with the correct intentions.

When a soul finally learns how to live the most moral incarnation they can live, when they bring their karmic balance to the positive, then they will be rewarded with salvation after their last death. For these souls, true salvation is the ability to stop being reborn, since being liberated from life is the real goal of reincarnation. This is the idea that the ancient teachers have handed down through the centuries. The modern view of reincarnation is that people come back because they want to, so they can complete something they failed to complete in their past life. They have indeed left unfinished business, but the souls do not come back of their own accord. They are told when to return to a new life. People believe in reincarnation to give them hope that life will go on after they leave the earth so that the next life does not seem so frightening. The idea of reincarnation gives you the chance to seek life after your current life has ended.

It is necessary to clear your karmic balance because you are not allowed to ascend to the astral plane until your karmic balance is on the positive side. There are many reasons for this. One of the most important reasons is that the inhabitants of the astral plane are the ones that people on earth seek guidance from. With your newly opened Third Eye, you have probably already sought advice from the inhabitants of the astral planes and other worlds. When you pursue this guidance, you want to know that it is coming from a reliable source and will be beneficial for you. This is why all of the souls that ascend to the astral plane will need to be pure and good.

Now that your Third Eye is open and functioning correctly, you can seek guidance and information from an infinite number of beings who have gone on before and who now inhabit the astral planes around you. These people are no further than a question away from you, and they now exist to help those on earth who need assistance gaining proficiency with their Third Eye and their new knowledge. As you are seeking information from the souls who have gone on before, you might encounter some beings that are at a higher level than most of the ascended beings you will encounter. These are the Ascended Masters who have finally moved beyond their physical incarnation and taken their rightful place in the astral world. These entities are more enlightened spiritually than most of the inhabitants of the astral plane, and they have fulfilled all of the physical incarnations they were required to perform. They will usually dwell in the highest dimension of the astral plane, the Fifth Dimension, but they are free to roam where they choose. As physical beings, they ascended to the rank of Healer, Shaman, Medicine Man, Master, Guru, or Yogi; they were people who were placed here with the ability to influence others. If you are lucky enough to know one of these people in their physical form, then know

CONCLUSION

Thank you for making it through to the end of *Kundalini*, let's hope it was interesting and informative and able to provide you with all of the tools you need to achieve your goals whatever they may be.

The next step is for you to begin your own journey toward spiritual enlightenment and astral awareness by taking the steps to awaken your Third Eye. This book has outlined the steps you can take and the methods that will help you as you move toward self-realization.

Awakening your Third Eye will give you the benefit of psychic powers that you can use to guide your life and make all things possible for you. It is easier to obtain the goals you have set for yourself when you have the wisdom and guidance of an infinite number or souls who have gone on before you. They are waiting on the astral plane, waiting to assist you with your psychic learning, but you will not be able to access their assistance until you awaken your Third Eye.

The path you walk will be uniquely yours, although others will be there to assist you. Use the information in this book to guide you along your path toward spiritual enlightenment and enrichment. You will not regret the choice.

Finally, if you found this book useful in any way, a review on Amazon is always appreciated!

that you are in the presence of one who will become an Ascended Master after they die. They have learned all of the lessons that were set for them to know, they cleared their karmic slate, and they are ready to move on to their next divine plan.

Ascended Masters are the best teachers for anyone on earth who is struggling to adjust to their Third Eye and the power it brings. They work from the realm of the spirits to assist the spiritual needs of those on earth. They will inspire and motivate your spiritual growth and acceptance. They want you to succeed, particularly in matters involving the Third Eye and your new abilities. Call on them any time you are in need.

If you take the time to become used to the power your Third Eye will bring, then you will eventually be able to use it effortlessly. Your Third Eye is your window to other worlds and other people. Now that it is opened, take the time to develop your abilities because they will take you far in your life.

www.ingramcontent.com/pod-product-compliance
Lightning Source LLC
Chambersburg PA
CBHW081346070526
44578CB00005B/737